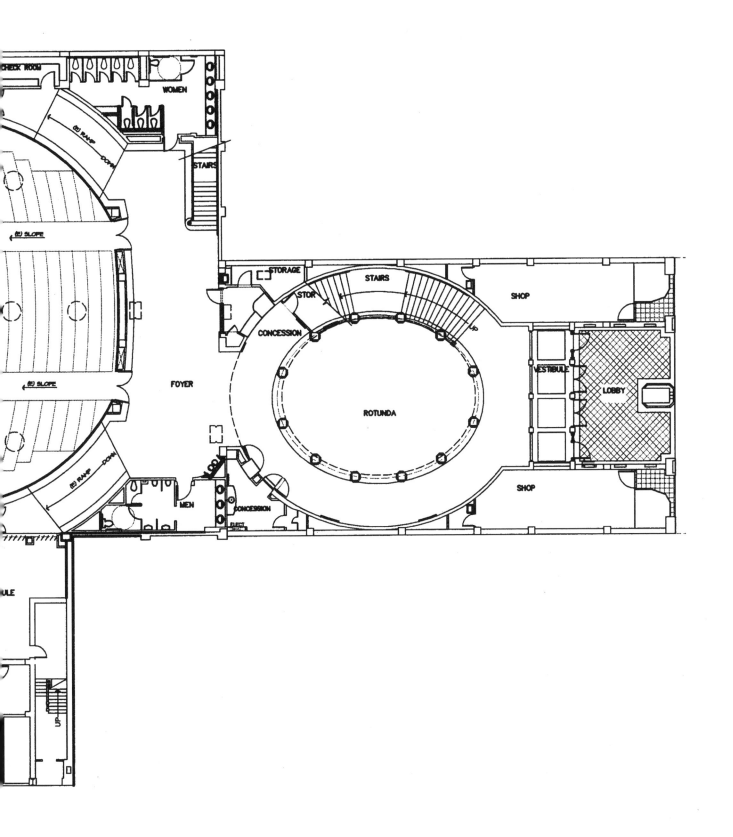

CHECK ROOM

WOMEN

(E) RAMP DOWN

(E) SLOPE

STAIRS

(E) SLOPE

FOYER

(E) RAMP DOWN

MEN

STORAGE

STOR

STAIRS

CONCESSION

SHOP

ROTUNDA

VESTIBULE

LOBBY

CONCESSION

ELECT.

SHOP

ULE

Stockton's Crown Jewel

The Bob Hope/Fox California

Stockton's Crown Jewel

The Bob Hope/Fox California

By

SYLVIA SUN MINNICK

With

ROBERT SHELLENBERGER

MARIAN VIEIRA STEVENSON

DON GEIGER

TOM BOWE

ROBERT HARTZELL

Friends of the Fox

Stockton, California

2005

Cover Design and Graphic Layout
By Snyder Lithograph
Dust Jacket Photos by Robert Canfield Photography
Layout preparation by
Sylvia Minnick and Eva Low
Editing: Del and Betty McComb
Archival research: Marian Vieira Stevenson
Memorabilia Collection: Jerry Sola, Jill Bennett Heard
Photography by: Robert Canfield, D. Thor Minnick,
Stephen Jester, Sylvia Minnick,
Robert Shellenberger, Jodee Samuelsen,
and Bob Price

Published by FRIENDS OF THE FOX
The Bob Hope/Fox California Theatre
242 East Main Street
Stockton, California 95202

The Friends of the Fox is a 501.c.3, non-profit organization. The purpose
of this limited publication is to commemorate the 75th anniversary of the
Bob Hope/Fox California Theatre in Stockton, California. The graphics came from
local institutions and private collections to which the organization is truly indebted.

———————

Library of Congress Catalog Number 2005929916

ISBN No. 0-9770552-0-5

Printed in Canada

Preface

*I*n 2002 the Bob Hope/Fox California $8.5 million dollar restoration began. At that time the affiliated, non-profit organization, Friends of the Fox mused about a book celebrating the theater's upcoming 75th anniversary – a Diamond Jubilee. It was two years later, in the late summer of 2004 that serious research began. The initial concept was to seek some oral interviews, add a few old photos, and throw in some statistics. This book was intended to be like other theater books describing the architectural elements of sweeping staircases, the brick-and-mortar dynamics of the building and include names for good measure. But, the research took on a life of its own and the original objectives became the lesser story.

Fortuitously, one contact led to another, one newspaper article led to more articles. Often, I saw smiles develop, eyes twinkle and a dreamy recollection of years-gone-by leap to the forefront. These were shared moments and very sacred. Most were definitely sentimental and passionate not only about the theater, but all the good the theater represented in their collective past as family and friends. The restoration has taken on a new civic pride not only for the theater but for downtown and for the city itself.

I cannot forget three very different and, yet, very thematic comments that set the tone for the future of the newly-renovated and newly-renamed The Bob Hope Theatre:

…In 1942 I thought the Fox was a wonderful theater like the Paramount in New York and other theaters in the big cities. Stockton really had an A-1 theater, much to my surprise. The grand re-opening in 2004 even made the Fox more beautiful than the first time I saw it…glittering and overwhelming.
> — *Olympe Bradna Wilhoit*

…When you set your mind to it, anything can happen. We, all, need to back the Fox and give it the support to make it work.
> — *Alex Spanos*

…Government saved it and the private sector will make it work. It will need all types of venues. This can be a generational thing. The county and the region are big enough to support everything here. Everyone wants a winner and when parents bring their families the children will remember when they become adults. Kids can get accustomed to going to the theater and repeat the pattern of teaching their children.
> — *Doug Wilhoit, Jr.*

Continued next page

Preface continued

It was clear, Stockton's Crown Jewel is not a conglomerate of architectural designs – the real jewel is found in today's spirit and memories of days gone by. Many adapted easily to its new name The Bob Hope; others tenaciously want to remember it as the Fox California.

Regardless, this is the history of a great lady. She became the only bright star in a world darkened by the October 1929 stock market crash followed by the desperation of a deep depression. It is estimated that over 20,000 people flocked to Main Street to witness the grand opening. They could not believe that their small city would have such a wonder. She offered the architecture, the gold-leaf columns, thick carpets, a winding grand staircase, the latest in sound, projection and, most importantly, the latest in air conditioning.

The theater was the sentinel which stood head and shoulders with the important buildings in downtown Stockton. She was a magnet as she attracted thousands from far reaches of the region. She was every family's babysitter as parents dropped off their children on Saturdays. Similar to the Statue of Liberty she was a symbol of strength and freedom serving as the center where soldiers and citizens flocked to participate in war bond rallies and viewed the latest exhibits put on by the War Department. She provided a magic carpet that allowed the ultimate in escapism, she was the reward for those who toiled and wanted a little time for respite.

A history of a community, a city and a people can be told through different venues. Not surprisingly, the Bob Hope/Fox California is the storyteller of Stockton's past and, perhaps, the predictor of Stockton's future.

S.S.M.

Table of Contents

Chapter 1
A Feast for the Eyes

After seventy-five years and three-plus years in renovation activities, one is struck when approaching the theater by the vision of an ornate tower rising like a large wedding cake above Main Street. The tower soars to a blue and yellow-clad cupola

Minnick Collection

Original small, wood-grained and gilded ticket booth

capped by an iron cruciform weather vane. It alludes to a Spanish colonial church without the requisite bell. It's the neon illuminated "FOX" blade sign and the flashing marquee that announces that it is not a mission, but rather "It's show time, folks!"

A newly-carved granite sidewalk hints of the long ago removed terrazzo sunburst-patterned walk that welcomed visitors. The inlaid bronze plaques are illustrative of a dropped glove, torn ticket stubs and, perhaps, a thrown rose dropped by a performer.

A small, wood-grained and gilded ticket booth welcomes the theater patron at the exterior lobby. Rust-colored terra cotta tiles highlighted with colored glass inserts of griffins, crosses and fleur-de-lis are seen underfoot. This exterior lobby is surrounded by gothic-arched poster cases announcing upcoming attractions. A gilt-metal and glass chandelier hangs from a coffered ceiling lighting the way to four pairs of wood and glass doors. Gold-leafed bas-relief plaster shields sit atop each pair of doors and, just below, plaster rope frames the gothic archways. The elements that make up this exterior lobby hint at an architectural smorgasbord of Gothic, Spanish colonial, classical Roman, Moorish and Renaissance elements with a bit of Hollywood thrown in for good measure.

Photographs from the Minnick Collection

The original drop-in safe is retained in the ticket booth.

Upon entering the theater, one is

transformed to another era walking through a gold-trimmed groin vaulted vestibule with its terrazzo floors bordered by deep red painted chevron patterned concrete floors. From the vestibule one enters the outer ring of the rotunda made up of twelve carved, plaster columns featuring carved faces in a myriad of sizes and expressions. These faces are encased in a lattice of gold-leaf plaster ribbons that rises to an ornate capital supporting the rotunda ceiling. The oval rotunda ceiling features thirty-six painted canvas panels, now wonderfully restored after the removal of many coats of red paint. The scenes are of conquistadors, heraldic shields, knights, squires and even lions. Cast-plaster, wood-grained panels which appear to be carved from ancient wood separate the illustrated canvas panels. Above these panels floats an oval-domed ceiling rimmed with gilded-swirling plaster molding representing

an evening sky in some far away place. At the center of the domed oval hangs a large, wedding cake-like, tiered, gold and silver leafed metal chandelier with over one hundred candlestick-like light bulbs. The illumination is majestic.

The outer walls of the rotunda are scored plaster simulating blocks of stone, thus, adding to the gothic qualities of the rotunda space. Hanging black iron chandeliers that appear to have once held bowls of fire as well as etched glass lensed recessed lights highlighted by a fleur-de-lis pattern add to the glow of the rotunda.

To the right or the west side of the rotunda a grand staircase curves its way up to the mezzanine level. Under-foot is multicolored patterned carpeting featuring medallions with red, blue and gold elements. Overhead, coffered ceiling canvas panels depict

Courtesy of WMB Architects | Robert Canfield Photography

The exquisite rotunda is made up of twelve carved, plaster columns featuring carved faces, encased in a lattice of gold-leaf plaster ribbons that rises to an ornate capital supporting the rotunda ceiling.

Courtesy of Stepen Jester

Rotunda chandelier with over 100-plus lights
lowered to check each bulb.

This space has been returned to a lounge area highlighted by a non-wood burning fireplace and carved-plaster beamed ceiling. A large north-facing window glazed with amber glass lets filtered light into the area. The plan is to use this lounge to house memorabilia of the theater's history as well as a biographic sketch of the theater's namesake – Bob Hope.

Returning once again to the main floor, one passes from the rotunda to a gilt-paneled flat arch into the lower foyer. Overhead are carved plaster, coffered, wood-grained panels that are highlighted with gold-striped accents. Situated between the two main set of doors to the auditorium, one is

botanical paintings of ancient plant life with curling vines and bursting seed pods.

Glancing down from the edge of the circular mezzanine railing with its wide, carved wood cap, one gets an overall view of a new marble mosaic art piece centered in the rotunda where once sat a bubbling, stepped fountain and pool. This hand-set mosaic features a large face blowing streams of water in swirling patterns that pay homage to the long removed fountain and to the waterfront so prominent in Stockton's history. As one walks slowly around the railing and gazes down to the mosaic below, one becomes captivated by the glitter of lights bouncing off the hundred-light chandelier.

Winding northward around the rotunda and flanked by the stone-like, patterned plaster walls, one ends at a lounge area just a few steps above the mezzanine level. This space, originally constructed as a smoking lounge, was later converted to a small theater space for the Hunter Square Players.

Minnick Collection

View from bottom of the rotunda chandelier.

struck by the beauty of six, eight foot tall, gold-leafed, carved plaster-framed, etched mirrored panels reminiscent of the Hall of Mirrors at Versailles Palace. A pair of carved wooden doors opens into the main auditorium. Once through the four entry portals and under the balcony level, one gets the first glimpse of the stage. Off the main floor foyer are the remodeled restrooms and another set of stairs to the west that leads to the mezzanine level.

The full impact of the auditorium's spaciousness is best realized from the mezzanine level. The

Minnick Collection

Eight foot tall, gold-leafed, etched-mirrored panels reminiscent of the Hall of Mirrors at the Palace of Versailles.

Courtesy of D. Thor Minnick

View looking out from the main foyer to the rotunda columns and outside doors.

Courtesy of D. Thor Minnick

Gilt-paneled flat arch in lower foyer with carved plaster, wood-grained panels. Also in view is one of two sets of doors leading into the auditorium.

when trying to absorb the interior's immenseness. The color palette is one of varied earth tones. A series of ornamental iron and amber glass chandelier and wall sconces provide sufficient lighting for the upper balconies. The coffered ceiling appears to be supported by the carved beams and these beams are elaborate and highlighted with gold leafing. The bottoms of the beams are stenciled with copper leaf in shades of green and burnt umber. Visually supporting these beams are oversized scrolling brackets featuring large-scale faces that allude to the classical comedy/drama masks of the ancient theater. A frieze, between the brackets, frames arch openings decorated with stenciled heraldic shields. Above these stenciled shields are large open-work, elaborately painted plaster panels. These panels act as screens for multi-colored indirect lighting.

mezzanine foyer space is highlighted by a wood-grained coffered ceiling that features gold-stenciled griffins. Cast iron chandeliers hang from the decorative ceiling. Other candle-like lights illuminate the stone-patterned walls.

Up a short set of stairs from the mezzanine foyer and through the maroon-colored velvet drapery panels, one enters into the auditorium at the balcony level. Standing there, a feeling of awe can be overwhelming

Facing the stage one sees first the outer proscenium arch with its hand-painted, sepia-toned mural of classical male figures astride galloping stallions in the clouds. The background of the arch includes a rose-colored sloping ceiling featuring a galaxy of gold, copper and silver stenciled stars suggestively directing one's eyes down to the main stage proscenium arch.

Courtesy of WMB Architects, Robert Canfield Photography

Mezzanine foyer highlighted by wood-grained, coffered ceiling. Center stairs lead to the balcony level.

A view of the proscenium arch with rose-colored ceiling featuring gold, copper and silver stenciled stars.
At the center of the arch is a shell-like halo encasing a large, gilded, carved face.

View of the organ loft.

Scrolling plaster detailing on the front of the proscenium arch comes to the center in a shell-like halo encasing a large, gilded, carved face. The background of the proscenium is stenciled in a checkerboard pattern of gold-leaf, stenciled stars and two-headed eagles. The stage is flanked on both sides with original hand-painted, plaster heraldic design elements. The main curtain is made of burgundy velvet trimmed with gold-colored, large bullion fringe.

On both sides of the stage are the organ loft chambers. Elaborate plaster moldings that simulate large window openings frame these chambers. The moldings curl over the top of the openings culminating in a gold-leafed shell with indirect illumination highlighting the stenciled copper, silver and gold stars above. These "window" openings are covered with canvas painting and allow the pipe organ music to waft through the fibers. These murals are reminiscent of 18th century pastoral scenes of people picnicking in a grove of eucalyptus trees. These murals were recreated in the New York studios of Evergreen Studios. At the lower portion of the organ chambers are simulated balcony fronts created from quilted velvet fabric panels with medallions highlighted in

A breath-taking view of the balcony.

gold thread. The sidewalls of the theater auditorium are scored in a simulated stone pattern found in the majority of the theater's interior walls.

The seats in the lower and loge portion of the theater are the original theater seats that have been refurbished with detailed, painted, end-panels and plush burgundy mohair fabric. The upper seats are recreations of the originals with the same level of detailing.

As one sits in the theater, one is engulfed in a myriad of architectural styles and elements. One is in some sort of far off place in a time long ago. These are elements that evoke a medieval castle with

Courtesy of D. Thor Minnick

Carved beams are highlighted with gold leafing. The bottoms of the beams are stenciled in copper leaf in shades of green and burnt umber.

Courtesy of D. Thor Minnick

A frieze, between the brackets, frames the arch openings decorated with stenciled heraldic shields.

Courtesy of WMB Architects, Robert Canfield Photography

One sees a myriad of architectural styles and elements in this full view of the audience chamber.

the simulated stone walls, stenciled heraldic shields and cast iron chandeliers. There is other cast plaster detailing that gives the illusion of being in a Moorish palace. It is difficult to place one definitive architectural style in the interior. Perhaps, the design being "over-the-top" in architectural detailing is meant to transport the audience to a fantasy land, just like the experience they have when watching a film.

From first glimpse of the theater's tower on Main Street to the procession through the two-story gilded rotunda, it is not hard to put oneself into the shoes of those first night patrons and join them in an evening of escape in this wonderful theater palace.

Tom Bowe

Chapter 2
Stockton:
A Great Theatre Town

*I*t is no surprise that Stockton boasts one of the grand movie palaces from the Golden Age of Cinema. Historically Stockton has been one of the great theater towns of California according to Mel Bennett, longtime editor of the *Stockton Record* and its theater critic for many decades.

Stockton, Sacramento and San Francisco were the big "show towns" of California's pioneer days. New York theatrical troupes sailed "around the horn" to San Francisco, traveled by steamboat to Stockton and Sacramento and then fanned out by wagon, carriage and horseback to entertain the miners in the mining towns of the Sierra Nevada.

Common lore avers that when western boomtowns blossomed, the men were immediately followed by saloons, gambling houses and "the girls." Formal entertainment, churches and schools came along in more settled times. While this general pattern began in Gold Rush California, the original Gold Rush population was not typical of later mining camps. Later camps were more likely made up of experienced miners seeking one more chance for quick riches. Stockton's Gold Rush population was spectacularly diverse. The men that flocked to California in '49 and '50 represented every profession, every trade, and every degree of education and sophistication. Doctor, lawyer, teacher, preacher, butcher, and farmer – they all came by the tens of thousands.

> *"The Stockton House hotel dining room was the site of Stockton's first theatrical production."*

California's 1847 non-Indian population rose from a mere 7,500 to 26,000 in a single year and then jumped to an astonishing 107,000 by December of 1849. Virtually all of this growth funneled through San Francisco and Sacramento and on to the "diggings". Stockton quickly became the supply and "jumping off" center for the Southern Mines. The California cities of importance after San Francisco were Sacramento, Stockton, and Marysville, eclipsing San Jose, and Monterey.

Prior to the Gold Rush, Stockton's founder, Captain Charles Weber, had a difficult time recruiting settlers from California's meager population for his little town of Tuleburg. The village totaled two log houses in 1847, and maybe twenty persons lived in all of what was to be San Joaquin County. Historian Frank Gilbert stated "Outside of Bonsell, Scott and Doak at the Ferry...there were four men, and not a woman or child in the county, outside of Stockton at that time, and in that town a small store. A small beginning for 1849."

Captain Weber joined his fellow Californians in heading for the Gold Fields almost immediately after the discovery was confirmed. He mined successfully on his own at Weber Creek, and then moved to open the Southern Mines, supplying his company with resources from Tuleburg. Successful at trading and collecting gold by use of Indians he had trained to mine, he was quickly able to give up these ventures and return to manage the growth of Tuleburg by September of 1848. His town was the natural jumping off location and supply source for all the Southern Mines. It was also strategically located on the main trail from San Jose to Sacramento. His town grew geometrically. J.H. Carson had passed through in 1848 and wrote about his return in 1849 "(the) Stockton I had last seen graced by Bussel's log house with a tule roof, was now a vast linen city."

The Captain resurveyed his city and renamed it Stockton. But, people were passing through, and not staying. There is no figure on Stockton's population at that point, but at least twenty men gathered at Christmas of 1848 to pool their resources to create a wassail bowl, the first known organized entertainment in Stockton. Soon after, it has been reported, a dance was announced and "well attended, but it broke up early, there being only one woman in attendance..." Later, a gambling tent of more than twenty tables was in operation and two girls were dealing Monte – a big draw.

By the end of 1849 Stockton had a permanent population of about 1,000 and a "floating" population of maybe 2,000. And then, on December 23, 1849, the linen city was destroyed by fire. The city was quickly rebuilt, this time with more wood structures. The first sermon was preached that same year. The first theatrical performance was in February of 1850.

Courtesy of Jill Bennett Heard

The Stockton Theatre, at the corner of Main and El Dorado Streets, opened on October 15, 1853, while the roof was still under construction. During its lifetime, it was constantly closed for repairs, and burned to the ground on July 4, 1890. It is pictured here in 1883 as Stockton's Admission Day Parade passed in the front.

Historian H.H. Bancroft said of the Stockton of 1849 –'50: "...it partook of the stirring phases of life characterizing the metropolis of this period, with gambling and drinking houses, dissolute and criminal excesses." It is certainly true that many a good young Christian Gentleman from Back East, separated from the puritan restraints of home and society for the first time, would go on a monumental binge of booze, cigars, faro cards, bear and bull fights, and fandangos, but the great majority of men were just achingly homesick for family and civil society. This nearly all-male population missed women most of all: wife, sweetheart, mother, sister, female companionship of all kinds. They would travel miles for a glimpse of a woman.

These voids were quickly filled. Show business entrepreneurs rushed to provide performers and plays to feed on the pent-up nostalgia of over 100,000 lonely men (and their gold). From the saucy Lola Montez to the plays of Shakespeare, success was immediate and profitable.

The Stockton House hotel dining room was the site of Stockton's first theatrical production. In 1850 a traveling acting company was formed in San Francisco and made its way to Stockton. With no stage and only sheets hung on wires for curtains, the players sold out the house with a well received performance of *Cox and Box*, a popular farce. The Stockton House hosted six more productions over the next few months and then gave way to the Corinthian Theatre. It was a primitive and meager effort, but theater was now an important part of Stockton's social fabric.

The Corinthian Building (or sometimes called the Corinthian Block), was a project of Captain Weber and Major Hammond. This three-story structure included a real theater of sorts on the third floor. Not missing a beat, the company that opened at the Stockton House, gave a final performance there on July 29, 1850 and opened the Corinthian three weeks later with a play called *Denouncer: or The Seven Clerks and Three Thieves*. Eight more shows followed before the end of the year, making a total of sixteen successful shows in 1850, Stockton's first theater season.

Stockton's first luxurious theater, the El Placer, arrived in 1851, bringing about the quick demise of the Corinthian. Built by a wealthy gambler, El Placer featured private boxes, cushioned seats, damask curtains and other amenities (including an "elegant" saloon). Total seating was 700 and two performances a week were promised. It opened February 11, 1851 and provided fourteen shows in the next few months before it was destroyed by the great fire of May 5, 1851. This fire was a true inferno. It totally devastated six square blocks of downtown Stockton, and destroyed 101 business properties, including the Stockton House. Stockton Theater would take a nine month intermission while the city recovered.

Drama returned February of 1852 by way of the Corinthian which escaped the fire. In its short second life, it offered fifteen plays over the next three months after which the local stage was dark until October of 1853. The entertainment void was filled with minstrel shows, circus, tableau vivant (models posed and unmoving in classic scenes – the females often naked!), pantomime, and similar passing variety shows.

The press reported the public was anxious for the return of real theater. Merchant Emile Hestra lost his store in the 1851 fire, but in rebuilding (with brick) he added an additional story to house a theater complete with iron shutters for fire protection. Dubbed the New Theatre, it boasted it was the "most chastely furnished and handsomely decorated hall of amusement in California." Additionally, the New Theatre was well equipped with curtains and back stage equipment. It became the heart of Stockton Theater for the next thirty years. The importance of theater entertainment in those early days can be best illustrated by noting John C. Fremont and his wife would endure the two-day buggy

ride from his mining property in Mariposa County to attend shows in Stockton.

The grand opening of the 700-seat house on October 15, 1853, was a major social event. The first offering was *Lady from Lyons*, a great favorite that had already been produced in Stockton at each of its three defunct theaters. The Chapman family, the premier acting company in northern California, presented it. The Chapmans offered fifty-two shows over the next three and a half months. On January 21, 1854, new management appeared and the theater name was changed to the Stockton. As the Stockton, the theater continued in operation until destroyed by fire in 1890.

During the first thirty years of operation this theater provided Stockton with the best entertainment available in California. A list of the artists who appeared on its stage included virtually every name performer of the era. Some of the names that can still be recognized today include Laura Keene, Harry Lauder, Madam Helen Modjeska, William F. "Buffalo Bill" Cody,

Bank of Stockton Archives

Lotta Crabtree, (1847-1924) a miner's daughter, began as a child performer in California's Mother Lode. She appeared in Stockton in 1853 at the age of six. She was more talented than her tutor, Lola Montez, and soon became America's favorite comedienne. Her final performance in Stockton was in 1890.

Lotta Crabtree, Fay Templeton, Captain Jack, and James O'Neil, father of playwright Eugene O'Neil. Additionally, it brought Stockton its first opera. The Stockton was Stockton's theater.

By 1882 Stockton was due for a new theater and construction of the Avon began. Originally dubbed The Grand Opera House, it featured gas lights, a huge lighted dome in lieu of overhead lamps, fancy seating for all but the gallery, (including "No. 1 opera chairs" in the grand circle), and a ladies' parlor. At the opening night gala, ladies received scented, satin-bound programs. Avon's opening play, *Hazel Kirk*, starred Effie Ellster. Management considered this a special event because it was the first and, perhaps, only show to play Stockton before San Francisco.

The Avon became everything the Stockton had once been. The very best of West Coast Theater played the Avon, including the best known performers of the

day. The opening of the Yosemite Theatre in 1892 stole away the major attractions, but the Avon soldiered on, providing a venue for boxing, minstrels, vaudeville, recitations, dog acts, amateurs and the like until 1902 when it bowed gracefully from the scene and was remodeled into a department store. One final gesture: on January 1, 1902, it featured a cineograph film showing the funeral of assassinated President McKinley, a portent of the future of theater entertainment in Stockton and everywhere.

Stockton Theater in its pioneer years was good theater for the times. There was no lack of professional talent, or theatrical companies. Salaries might be as low as $7.00 per week for ordinary players and maybe $100.00 for name leads. A Troupe might not travel with a full cast and would fill minor roles with local talent. Rehearsals were considered an insult by the old

Courtesy of Jill Bennett Heard

The Avon, at the corner of California and Main Streets, opened on August 14, 1882. The arched main entrance, visible at the lower right, was on California Street. The theater's 800-seat gallery was reached via stairway entrance on Main Street.

Bank of Stockton Archive

The Yosemite Theater, 25 North San Joaquin Street, opened on July 12, 1892 with a performance by Maude Adams in *The lost Paradise*. Demand for tickets was so high that they were auctioned off a week before. Dress circle seats went for $22.50, orchestra seats at $5 and $6, or three times the regular price. The Yosemite closed in June of 1919.

pros of the road. In the 1850s, Laura Keene would tour with only her manager, costumes and perhaps a leading man and count on the community to provide scenery and cast. Companies would often present as many as six or seven different plays in as many nights. Keeping "up" on so many parts put enormous pressure on the players and made the prompter an important member of each company. The completion of the transcontinental railroad in 1869 made it easier for eastern talent to tour the west, and the stars of New York became increasingly available for West Coast productions.

The opening of the Yosemite Theatre in 1892 marked the beginning of the Golden Age of legitimate theater in Stockton. It was perfectly designed for play production and the vaudeville shows that loomed in its future. Theater historian Mel Bennett described it as "…high, wide and handsome – high to accommodate the lower floor, a two-section balcony and a gallery; wide and shallow, the better to see and hear." Total seating capacity was 1325, yet it seemed "intimate." It

was a great favorite of touring companies and a major reason they often described Stockton as a "great theater town." It was handsomely decorated and the first Stockton theater to be totally lighted by electricity (one of the first in the West) complete with stage dimmers. Its eight box seats were great favorites of local ladies anxious to show off the latest styles of dress.

The grand premier show was *The Lost Paradise* starring a young Maude Adams, already well on her way to stage stardom. Miss Adams routed her touring show especially for this event. The audience gave her a standing ovation.

The Yosemite arrived in time for the beginning of the age of the "Road." At the beginning of the Twentieth Century, a good Broadway run might be as little as a season or a year. Economics demanded that a successful run follow with a road tour of a year or more, complete with original cast. Thus, the best of Broadway made its way to Stockton and local fans were treated to appearances by the greatest talent in the land. Stockton

Courtesy of Kathleen Bennett Johnson

ETHEL BARRYMORE, whose career began on the stage, played at the Yosemite Theatre in 1907 and 1909. Much later, after years in films, she returned to the stage at the University of the Pacific Auditorium in the 1940s to perform in *The Corn is Green*.

had always attracted virtually the same performers and plays that appeared in San Francisco, but never in the numbers available during the age of the "Road."

According to Glen Kennedy, in 1900 there were over 400 stock and dramatic companies on tour plus minstrels, opera, vaudeville and burlesque companies. Stockton could pick and choose from a cornucopia of entertainment.

Indicative of the stature of the Yosemite and Stockton as a theater town was the billing of the gigantic presentation of *Ben Hur* in 1905. The Yosemite manager brought the huge production to Stockton for a three day, 4-performance stand. It was widely advertised and promoted. Result? An estimated 5,000 people – 2,000 from out of town – attended in a theatre that seated only 1325.

Some of the performers who played the Yosemite in this Golden Age included Maude Adams, who opened the Yosemite in 1892, and Ruth Chatterton and Henry Miller who closed it in 1919. Between these events the Yosemite hosted W.C. Fields, Otis Skinner, Jack Benny, Fred Allen, the Marx Brothers, Sir Harry Lauder, George M. Cohan, The Barrymores (Ethel, Lionel, and John), Lillian Russell, John Philip Sousa and his band, Sophie Tucker, Will Rogers, and dozens more, many well remembered nearly a century later. Some, like W.C. Fields were on their way up, some, like Lillian Russell, were near the end of their careers. It didn't matter. Stockton met them all, walking on its streets, dining in its restaurants, and on the Yosemite stage.

Changing economics and the arrival of the movies brought an end to the old Yosemite in 1917. Its shell would live on until 1971, but it was not the same. The Queen was dead and the Stockton entertainment scene continued without a monarch until the debut of the spectacular Fox California in 1930.

While the local entertainment scene was always dominated by a single theater, many acts that could not afford a first class theater or were unsuitable for a normal stage setting found other venues. Minstrel shows (black-faced, black, and mixed companies) were very popular, but there seemed to be more minstrels than play houses. There was the circus, of course. Shows that found

This stately pavilion, built in 1887, located on East Washington Street, covered the entire block across from old St. Mary's Church. It was Stockton's first auditorium. In its time, the pavilion accommodated agricultural fairs, stage shows, concerts, dances and other events requiring larger quarters. The Royal

Bank of Stockton Archives

Hawaiian Band performed there in 1895. It burned to the ground in 1902 in a conflagration that took the life of a firefighter and consumed the entire city block.

Courtesy of Kathleen Bennett Johnson

AL JOLSON made several appearances in Stockton. He played at the Yosemite in 1917, at the T & D in *Sinbad* in 1920, and at the State in 1929. His landmark 1929 film, *The Jazz Singer*, included his memorable renditions of *Mammy* and *Toot Toot Tootsie.*

other homes included many second rate variety shows, pantomimes, panoramas, gymnasts, magicians, bell ringers, electrical demonstrations, recitations, lecturers like Carrie Nation, glass blowers, artist's models, dog and monkey shows, and similar opportunities for amusement at a small price.

The older theaters struggled on hosting these acts, but many found homes in the Masonic Hall, Weber Baths, Madden's Music Hall, public buildings, dance halls, etc. One notable alternative was the Agricultural Pavilion located on Washington Square. It was erected in 1887-88 to house the county fair. It was Stockton's first great auditorium and the biggest building in the city at 38,000 square feet. In addition to its fair duties, it was home to political rallies, balls, lectures, and traveling shows. It was destroyed in a great fire in 1902.

The American motion picture evolved from the combined genius of Thomas A. Edison and George Eastman. Eastman provided flexible film and Edison did the rest. Moving picture experiments were also underway in Europe. At a demonstration in Paris in 1895, August Lumiere stated, "Our invention can be exploited for a certain time as a scientific curiosity, but part from that, it has no commercial future whatsoever." Edison knew better.

One authority noted that the very first movies were actually mini-documentaries. Typical content would be a cattle drive, boat race, arrival of the fleet, funerals and public ceremonies. *The Great Train Robbery*, which ran nine minutes, was the first commercial movie with a plot. By summer of 1903, Novelty Park, an open-air theater, showed movies along with vaudeville regularly, as did the open-air dance hall in Oak Park. The

Novelty, at 335 E. Weber Avenue, also featured movies and vaudeville and was followed by the Unique at 27 North Sutter Street in 1904. It began with road shows, a stock company, and vaudeville. This schizophrenic theater became the Empire in 1906, the Alisky in 1907, the Forest in 1908, the Garrick in 1909, the first Hippodrome in 1911, the Strand in 1915, and then the Hippodrome again, and finally the Strand yet again! Nearly every movie theater in Stockton underwent at least one name change during its active life.

These name changes reflected changes in ownership and management philosophy as business tried to find audiences in an atmosphere of change. Road companies were losing out to vaudeville and the "flickers."

The first theater built in Stockton especially for movies was the Idle Hour at 26 North Sutter Street in 1910. It was well named because the average movie was either a two or three reeler. Each reel averaged twenty minutes. Your dime generally bought you one hour of entertainment. The Idle Hour was also the first to feature a Wurlitzer organ in lieu of what was already the tradition of tinkling piano accompaniment for the silents.

While the moviemakers were learning their craft, Stockton continued to host the best of the road shows and vaudeville. After 1910, road shows became scarce and harder to book. But vaudeville was in its prime. The policy was three acts of vaudeville and one movie, both accompanied by a four-piece orchestra. Most of the others had a similar regime. The Yosemite booked the Orpheum vaudeville circuit for many years, usually on Sunday and Monday, and thus, the theater was known as the Orpheum two days a week. This show was strictly eight acts of the very best entertainers. In later years the Orpheum acts were booked by the State.

Between 1903 and 1930 Stockton saw Burns and Allen, Jack Benny, Fred Allen, Fred and Adele Astaire, Fanchon and Marco reviews, the Ziegfeld Follies, Ethel Waters, Trixie Friganza, W.C. Fields, Sophie Tucker, Al Jolson, The Marx Brothers, The Stooges (later the Three Stooges), Ed Wynn, Victor Moore, and dozens more. John Phillip Sousa came to town nearly every year with his band.

As vaudeville died, the movies quickly grew longer and better. The first authentic film star was Bronco Billie Anderson. In fact the cowboys dominated early movies even if the pictures were forgettable. William S. Hart, Tom Mix, the Gish sisters, Harry Carey, Buck

Courtesy of Jill Bennett Heard

THE NOVELTY THEATRE, a vaudeville house at 335 East Weber, opened on November 22, 1903, featured "monologists" (today's standup comics), acrobats and ragtime singers. Al Jolson recalled that the stage entrance was gained through the kitchen of the next door tamale house.

Jones, and Dustin Farnum are some remembered from the days of the silent "oaters".

Stockton's theaters in the teens and early twenties included the Colonial (formerly the Yosemite), the venerable (and seedy) Stockton, the State, Lincoln, Lyric (became the National in 1924), Rialto and Strand. As can be seen, the swirling confusion of name changes continued, but the theaters remained the same, all confined to Stockton's downtown theater district.

In 1917 Stockton was graced by a new, first rate theater with the construction of the T & D on Main Street. It was built to host both road shows and movies. One road show included Al Jolson in *Sinbad* in 1921. This was at least the third appearance in Stockton by Jolson, who dubbed himself "The world's greatest entertainer." Other popular shows included a series of Marcus Reviews (which included leggy chorus lines), and most memorably, *The Passing Show* of 1922 which featured 200 singers and dancers, 3,300 costumes, twenty six colossal sets, and stars Gene and Willie Howard. In 1923 the T & D became The California.

Stockton was past due for a palace of its very own. Patrons wanted a twinkling marquee,

Courtesy of Jill Bennett Heard

THE GARRICK THEATRE, at 21 North Sutter, underwent several names changes. Initially called the Hippodrome, then the Unique, the Garrick, the Strand, later the Strand-Hippodrome and finally back to simply called the Hippodrome.

THE LYRIC THEATRE, 124 North Sutter, opened in 1913, complete with a balcony, a pipe organ, upholstered seats, color lighting and a rudimentary air-conditioning system. It was described as the forerunner of the movie palaces of the 1930s.

MDE. SCHUMANN-HEINK, 1861-1936, appeared at the "Auditorium" in January 1920, to an estimated 1300 people. The overflow crowd sat on the stage. "Madame," as she was known, made her operatic debut at 17, became an American citizen in 1905, and despite strong ties to Germany, entertained US troops. In July of 1917, she was decorated with the colors of the 21st Infantry Division and made an honorary colonel. In November 1921, prior to giving another concert at the Auditorium, she participated in the dedication ceremonies of Radio Station KWG, then housed in the Stockton Record Building.

lavish lobby, uniformed ushers to show them to their seat, and, of course, first class entertainment. It happened in 1929 when Stockton's newest and largest theater, the California was leveled and construction of the Fox theatre began. It proved a treat worth waiting for, because the result was as fine a theater as any city in California could boast. Whether it was called The Fox, The California, The Fox-California, or the Fox-California Bob Hope, it grandly assumed the crown as the new queen of entertainment for Stockton – A Great Theater Town.

Robert Shellenberger

– 20 –

Chapter 3
A Stockton Wonder

The late Dr. Coke Wood wrote in his book, *Stockton Memories* (1977), "*The history of a community can almost be told in terms of the important buildings that have been erected over the years, especially public and semi-public buildings. This history is written in bricks, stones, building materials with the labor, skill and pride of the people in the community.*" This statement could not be truer than in the city of Stockton as she entered the decade of the 1920s. Her citizenry, whose population reached 56,000, had seen the end of World War I and the dreaded Spanish Influenza of 1918. Even with those major devastating events, her citizenry was cloaked in optimism.

Stockton's skyline had already begun to change with the construction of the Mission Revival style Hotel Stockton in 1910. This block-long, 200-room hostelry at the head of the channel was easily a landmark building; no, it was *the* signature of the city. A building boom in the downtown buoyed the business atmosphere particularly at the intersection of Main and San Joaquin Streets. At the northeast corner stood the

Jerry Sola Collection

MAIN STREET, circa 1925

seven-story Stockton Savings and Loan Society Building, with a bank on the ground floor and the Yosemite Club on the top floor. On the opposite southwest corner the Farmers and Merchants Bank opened in 1917; and since it was newer it had to be taller, topping at nine stories. The Commercial and Savings Bank, just a block to the east at Main and Sutter Streets was another high rise built the previous year. Clearly, the Main Street corridor fully intended to be the center of the financial district as well as the heart of the city.

Jerry Sola Collection

FARMERS & MERCHANTS BANK stands at the corner of San Joaquin and Main Streets. This photo provides a glimpse of the T & D Theatre to the right.

When the 1920s decade began, Stockton took on an even greater construction boom. The new Masonic Temple broke ground at the intersection of Market and Sutter Streets in 1921; in almost simultaneous order city fathers ordered the building of a new City Hall and Civic Memorial Auditorium. Both buildings were dedicated in 1926. The following year the Medical-Dental Building added to Stockton's skyline as did several multi-story apartment buildings well within the downtown area. In step with the 1920s spirit, Stockton Unified School District made additions to Elmwood, Jackson, Stockton High and Wilson schools. This was also the time when McKinley (1922) Victory (1923) Roosevelt (1923) Burbank(1925) and addition to Lottie Grunsky (1927) were built. Even farther north of the city limits, College of the Pacific relocated from San Jose and built their campus.

Stockton clearly demonstrated it was a city that wanted to move forward in finance, education and cultural institutions. Recreational activities included the building of the Stockton Country Club. The city was also prepared to enter the "golden age" of motion pictures with twenty movie theaters, four vaudeville houses plus several large capacity-seating auditoriums to draw in the celebrities of Hollywood and Broadway.

In 1916 Roley E. Wilhoit, President of Stockton Savings and Loan Bank, had astutely invested $150,000 in a theater half a block west of his office on Main Street. His second son George negotiated the land transaction. The theater abutted the Farmers & Merchants Building on a lot size of one hundred by three hundred feet, its address 242 East Main Street, and its name the T & D Photoplay. These initials stood for Turner and Dahnken, former owners of the theater. While this first-run movie house had a Wurlitzer organ and full management including usherettes, it faced stiff competition from the other theaters. The T & D underwent two name changes, first to the California Theater and then in 1921, when the Fox West Coast Theaters organization leased the theater, the name changed to the Fox California. Everyone still called it the T & D.

Roley E. Wilhoit died in 1922 and the Stockton Savings and Loan Bank presidency passed on to Eugene L. Wilhoit, his eldest son. Even though the theater received some remodeling in 1924, it was only a matter of time when the Fox officials caught the pervasive financial optimism of the town's people and matched the other building activities. As Eugene Wilhoit stated, "That $150,000 building could be torn down after little more than a decade shows the tread of the times. The original building which housed the old California Theater was good, but the Fox West Coast people did not think it was good enough for Stockton."

Bank of Stockton Archives

ROLEY E. WILHOIT, president of Stockton Savings and Loan Bank, bought the land that housed the T & D Theatre.

While in 1929 the property inclusive of land, building, equipment and furnishing was valued at one million dollars, the Fox West Coast Theaters,

EUGENE L. WILHOIT, spearheaded the move to demolish the T & D Theatre to make way for the Fox California in 1929. Wilhoit succeeded his father, Roley E. Wilhoit as president of the Stockton Savings and Loan Bank.

MAMIE W. HODGKINS, sister of Eugene Wilhoit, owned one quarter share of the land leased to the Fox West Coast Corporation.

ELSIE W. HODGKINS, sister of Eugene and Mamie, also owned one quarter share of the land.

Inc.'s vision was to raze the old theater and build a new structure which incorporated state-of-the-art technology within the industry. The Fox West Coast organization was prepared to lay out a heavy investment to build an architectural wonder befitting not just a central valley town but one that served as a magnet of entertainment for several surrounding communities. Serious negotiations began that year between Eugene Wilhoit and the Fox corporation. The end result was a fifty-year lease with the Wilhoit Family that ran from July 1, 1929, until May 31, 1979. The property was in the names of the surviving Roley Wilhoit's children: eldest son Eugene L., third son Arthur, and daughters Elsie Wilhoit Hodgkins and Mary Wilhoit Hodgkins. The second son, George had already died. These four each shared one quarter of the land lease.

Eugene Wilhoit proved that he was as astute a businessman as his father in that he required Fox West Coast, Inc. to secure a bonded indebtedness for $300,000, financed through a trust indenture to Stockton Savings and Loan Bank which also served as the trustee. This allowed the bank to sell bonds at a rate of 5.5% for a twenty-five year term ending July 28, 1944.

The deadly flu pandemic of 1918-1919 eventually killed more than twenty million people. By order of the Board of Health, theaters, schools and other public gathering places were closed from October 18 through November 23, 1918 and were ordered closed again in January 1919. Facemasks were required by law and are visible on this group of people watching a parade along Main Street, with the T & D marquee visible on the left.

Such a transaction would not be possible with today's banking laws and oversight regulations. Given that all the transactions and bond sales occurred almost five months before the great market crash, the investment was sound. As Eugene L. Wilhoit pointed out, "The old California theater building…was a satisfactory investment by reason of the trustworthiness and ambition of the Fox West Coast organization and its management." With the financing in place, the project proved to be a salvation for many workers during the hard hit depression years.

Stockton's Department of Building Inspection on September 16, 1929, issued Permit #7683 to the Fox West Coast Theaters and the contractor Bellers Construction Company to build a theater. It was estimated to cost $240,000 and the fee charged was $96.00. As Vickie Lee Benton succinctly indicated in her paper of May 1974:

> The architects were Balch and Stanberry of Los Angeles, and the general contractor, who was granted a bond of $359,000, was Beller Construction Company of Hollywood. All the electrical wiring was done by a local wiring contractor, Edward L. Gnekow, on a bond of $32,000. Gillespie and Tinkham, Inc., a local company, installed the heating and ventilating system on a bond of $42,000. The building with furnishings represented an expenditure of $500,000, of which $200,000 was spent locally. The $200,000 expenditure and the weekly payroll, which exceeded $3,000, helped Stockton weather the depression.

As Stocktonians watched the razing of the old T & D, they assumed the building of the new Fox would be a long, slow process even though Fox management projected the grand opening of the new theater for October of the same year. This would be in less than ten months. Foremost to the project was audience safety followed by courtesy and comfort as part of the services to be offered. Howard Sheehan, vice president of the Fox West Coast organization, commented that "The intent is to make the Stockton Fox Theater an ultra-modern theater of magnificence and comfort equal to any theater in the country." Sheehan then

City of Stockton Files

The original Building Permit was issued on September 16, 1920. A $96 fee paid for the issuance of the permit to construct the new Fox California at the estimated cost of $240,000. Work began in January 1930.

promised that Fox will "build Stockton a theater that ranks with the foremost playhouse in the country and one that will long be one of the show places in the San Joaquin valley." No details in the entire structure would be neglected and all equipment would be of the best quality obtainable. When completed it would be one in a chain of thirty-two Fox movie palaces in California.

Stocktonians did not realize that Fox was simultaneously planning the construction of a movie palace farther down the valley in Bakersfield and that the city of Oakland's Paramount Theater was also on the drawing board and projected to open the following year. Actually it did not matter for the locals had enough good vibes about their own upcoming theater.

Almost weekly and even daily as construction began, readers of the local newspaper followed the progress. An architectural concept of Spanish mission design included a tower that set the building apart from its surrounding. An inspiring foyer with a bubbling fountain led to a grand stairway up to a winding balcony supported by mammoth pillars. Massive beams of natural wood supported the ceiling and gave the

FOX CALIFORNIA THEATRE JOB DAY BY DAY BUILDER'S LOG BOOK

January (1st week)	Cement pouring began
Jan. 26	Structural steel men on the job, a week later the bricklayers appeared.
Jan. 28	Workmen formed the rotunda roofs and walks; 3 days later riveting began on the balcony girder.
Feb. 17	Erection of steel frame in the tower that graces tower front
Feb. 27	Organ loft being framed
March 7	Still working on big truss, getting ready for fireproofing
March 24	Fifty-two sacks of cement used in pouring the fountain in the rotunda
April 24	Painters started working on the tower
May 7 (Sat.)	Three men worked in the afternoon, taking cement used as a weight test off the balcony
June 11	Forty-five sacks of cement used for rat-proofing the air ducts, work began grading the musicians' room
June 18	Truck loaded with 2x4 to be used in construction of the Fox West Coast theater in Bakersfield
June 25	Plasters went to work on the organ lofts, auditorium ceiling and proscenium arch
July 1	Portholes in the projection room completed and door jamb set in the ticket booth
July 9	Decorators at work in lobby and rotunda
July 15	The organ was unloaded to be installed tomorrow (7/16)
July 28	Money drawers and ticket chopper were set in the ticket booth
Aug. 13	Sheet metal men to complete the marquee; electricians working on the switchboard; ventilator men setting mushrooms in auditorium and balcony floor; lumber loaded out on truck headed for Bakersfield.
Aug. 18	Generator motors set
Aug. 25	Inspector okayed roof
Aug. 29	All men laid off except one carpenter and three laborers
Sept. 13	Construction company turned the completed building over to seat men, carpet men and electric fixture men.
Oct. 11	Nick Turner, local Fox West Coast manager arrived at his office and found tons of carpet for the new theater awaiting his signature
Oct. 14	Date set for opening.

Stockton Daily Independent
October 12, 1930

auditorium an air of ancient artistry, particularly with motif designs similar to European crests. Lighting fixtures hanging between the beams produced a soft rosy effect to contrast the light-colored beige walls with that of the décor and the plush colorful carpets imported from the Far East.

The main auditorium sat over 1500, the loge section another 500 seats and an upper balcony held yet another 220. All the new seats installed were the most luxurious in design and similar to those in the San Francisco Fox Theatre, then considered the finest theater in the world. Some aisle seats had special ear

phone plugs to benefit the hearing impaired. The advent of talking pictures left thousands of deaf persons without the ability to enjoy fully motion picture entertainment; thus, the theater industry wishing to accommodate these people, as did the Fox, wired special amplification plugs into the side panel of the seats. Each phone had its own dial, similar to a radio receiving set. Headsets were available for a two dollar deposit per showing with the understanding that the devices be returned.

The original Wurlitzer pipe organ from the old T & D was reinstalled with twin pipe lofts on either side of the stage. The stage configuration measured seventy feet high, ninety feet across and thirty feet deep. The auditorium constantly was filled with fresh air filtered through a screen of water, and the latest and best heating and cooling system was installed. The air conditioning machinery used to ensure the constant temperature is capable of making one hundred and twenty tons of ice daily. Lounging rooms at the end of the winding balcony and parlors for the patrons held modern but comfortable furniture, intending as a contrast to bring out the ancient designs which formed the motif of the theater.

The door to the projection room was accessible from the last aisle in the balcony and within this room were three enormous projectors and a commode. Nearby the generator produced enough current to light fifteen homes and with only a slight modification and the addition of a proper vacuum tube the sound equipment could be transformed into a highly efficient radio broadcasting station. The projection room was absolutely fireproof having automatic fire shutters which closed the portholes in case of a film fire, a separate ventilation system would take the smoke out of the building. Sprinkler heads would melt if a certain temperature is reached and release a powerful spray of water. Simultaneously, an alarm would sound at the fire station and the house lights in the theater would turn themselves on so the crowd could exit the building safely. There are twelve exits so arranged that no seat is farther than forty-five feet from the nearest exit. Meanwhile the projectionist had an escape hatch which would allow him to leave the building via the roof. The

Courtesy of Jill Bennett Heard

Scene in front of the Fox, circa 1930s

committee decided to have an open air fete to handle the overflowing crowds who would not be able to get tickets on opening night but wanted to share in the excitement. At most, only about 5,000 lucky individuals could claim they saw the opening night two performances and the last stragglers would not be out of the theater until well past midnight. Thus the initial plans included erecting a platform at Hunter Plaza, scheduling several vaudeville acts and, perhaps, even drawing movie stars from Hollywood. Bert Lewis served as master of ceremonies at the Hunter plaza attraction and Henry Cunningham was in charge of the formal dinner dance at the Hotel Stockton after the show. This was going to be a black tie affair and even was described as the "biggest social affair in Stockton since before the beginning of the War." The Karl Ross American Legion Post drum corps would start the festivities at 7:00 p.m. with a march down Main Street to the square where they would execute difficult and colorful routines. Planners envisioned special guests driving up in long limousines pulling up in front of the Fox, their grand entrance illuminated by the bright Kleig lights.

entire structure is built of steel trusses and the plates have special fire-proof material covering.

By October 12, 1930, a simple and short FOX sign was erected, and even though the full name was Fox California, builders felt the fewer letters made the sign more legible at a greater distance. With the major project almost fully completed the *Stockton Daily Independent* published the project manager's log book showing the amazing speed, coordination, and details associated with the construction. By then planning for the grand opening was in full swing

The City Council, at the end of September, pledged financial support for the grand opening and assigned a committee composed of prominent businessmen and local leaders. They were Ray Friedberger, Fred R. Schneider, Jr., Henry Glick, Ben Ganeles, Deane Hobson, Mrs. W. A. Fitzgerald, Dick Downs, John Dinubilo, Henry Cunningham, Will Dunne, Bert Lewis, A.B. Cohn, Eugene Wilhoit and A. M. Robertson with Mr. Schneider as chairman. The

Rumors flew that the price of admission was going to go as high as $5.00 but Fox management quickly assured that the opening night price would be that of the regular price of fifty cents for all seats except sixty cents for loges. Theater manager Nick Turner stated: "Our theater is to serve the whole public and while we expect to make the opening of the new Fox California Theater a memorable event in the theatrical history of this section of the State, there will be no reserved seats on the big opening night and our regular prices will prevail." He made the statement while discussing plans for the opening. The local newspaper found this democratic innovation refreshing as "in the past, it has been the regular custom throughout the country to charge special prices for big opening events and to reserve seats far in advance." The article continues, "Mr. Turner is setting an admirable example here in this attitude that the theater is built for all the public and that no distinction either in prices or reserved seats shall deprive anybody of an opportunity to enjoy the opening that Stockton folks have so long wanted." At the same time Fox announced the opening night lineup with a feature movie starring Spencer Tracy.

Adjoining the Fox article, an advertisement announced that the Hunter Plaza program, sponsored by the Business Men's organization, would start at 7:00 p.m. with twelve big vaudeville acts, a thirty-piece band, dancing, radio stars in person, music by Maurice Gunsky, the Karl Ross Post Drum Corps and Glee Club and much more.

Excitement began to build with daily reports in the newspapers. Even the San Joaquin Pioneer and Historical Society's women auxiliary got into the act. They invited the oldest pioneers from the Mother Lode, Tracy, and the surrounding communities as honored guests. These senior citizens would dine at the Stockton Hotel and by 7:00 p.m. be escorted to the loge seats set aside for them. The hope was

that these sagacious persons would approve of modern amenities and that the entertainment forthwith "may be considered a proclamation that the world is still a good place to live and that happiness may still be secured in the day's endeavor." This comment in the press attempted to mitigate the mood of the community regarding the rough times created by the Depression. Clearly, movies from Hollywood were important to the human psyche for it took one into a world of fantasy, if only for a few hours. In retrospect, if there was one disappointment for these senior citizens in this grand affair, it was that there was no elevator. To reach their special seating they had to climb up the flight of stairs to reach the mezzanine and then descend numerous

steps to their appropriate rows overlooking the stage. The best intentions of the day addressed the hale and hearty and did not account for the infirmities that often afflicted the elderly. Since there were no comments in the newspapers by these special guests after the grand opening it is assumed the evening went off without any problems.

The Traction Company, an electric streetcar that ran between Lodi and Stockton, agreed to delay their last car run of the evening another thirty minutes, until 10:30 p.m. so that Lodians could come to Stockton for the opening. Opening night plans included installing twelve loud speakers so that the ceremony could be heard throughout the area. Sirens, signals, whistles and bells prepared to be blown at five-thirty to let people know of the doors' opening. Bert Lewis, secretary of the Downtown Association, was prepared to announce the arrival of movie stars and other notables.

OPENING NIGHT – OCTOBER 14, 1930

The morning *Stockton Record*'s editorial enthusiastically gave accolades for promises kept by Fox West Coast management. A reporter's early inspection testified that they had indeed built Stockton a first-class movie palace. The comment, "there is a tendency of big theatrical syndicates to assume the attitude that anything will do outside of the big centers – was quite the contrary here. Only the very best of everything has been provided….As a result of this generous attitude the Fox California is as fine a house as can be found in the State outside of San Francisco and Los Angeles." The Fox "embodied the best in design, beauty and comfort and people have reason to celebrate. The opening is worthy of a gala celebration, very public in character."

To promote the importance of Hollywood, the *Stockton Record* stated, "Excellent and varied entertainment takes men and women away from the humdrum of daily lives. Screen dramas give them the color and romance that they have missed. All this is done at the popular prices that put the picture house

within reach of millions, whereas only thousands went to the theater in the old lamented days."

Also on the same opening day the *Stockton Daily Independent* commented, "The Fox California in maintaining its regular prices for its grand opening is evincing a fine democratic spirit – one that its patrons will greatly appreciate. Community celebration on Hunter Plaza providing for all large crowds throughout the evening is most appropriate and speaks of a 'community observance.'"

Local merchants took out advertisements congratulating the Fox, giving their full enthusiastic support to the grand event. Among these merchants were: Wilson-Schultz & Company, The Electrical House; Hunter Square Café; El Dorado Brewing Company, Turner Hardware; Oyster Loaf Grill and Delta Ice Cream Company. Main Street and Weber Avenue took on an air of celebration. Downtown merchants decorated their storefronts, put up flags and kept their store lights on during opening night. After five o'clock, parking was prohibited between Market and Weber Streets, Main Street was closed off to traffic between San Joaquin and El Dorado Streets. However, parking was allowed along the curb and down the center of Miner Avenue, two blocks to the north of the Fox. The

Bank of Stockton Archives

A night scene of Main Street taken at night during the holiday season. Circa 1937.

police were out in force for violators. The plaza was roped off, washed, waxed and powdered for dancing and entertainment. High-powered footlights, strings of olivets overhead and three Kleig lights lit the front of the theater and lights stretched the entire block to Hunter Plaza. Powerful searchlights spanned the sky over the courthouse dome and building tops. A special fire patrol patrolled the theater area because of all the electrical fixtures in use.

The grand opening met Stockton's expectations. People started to line up at 2:30 p.m. for the 5:30 door opening, each wanting to be a part of the $500,000 movie palace dedication. Shortly after the doors opened the crowd grew to such capacity it broke through the police restraints to enter the theater.

At 5:45 p.m. Mrs. Inez McNeil formally dedicated the organ and performed a solo. Mrs. McNeil, a Stockton resident for twenty-two years, was the original organist of the old T & D. She was credited with having one of the largest libraries of organ music in the state. One of her young pupils was George Wright, who became an organist-par-excellence and was world renowned.

First on the cinema program was *UP THE RIVER*, a dark humor Fox production starring Spencer Tracy, Warren Hymer, Claire Luce, William Collier, Sr., Humphrey Bogart and others. And in quick succession the audience saw a newsreel, travel log about Hong Kong, and an animal talkie entitled "Hot Dog." After the showings local attorney Warren H. Atherton gave an oral description of the theater. A number of dignitaries including a large contingent from Fox were introduced. Mayor Carl J. Tremain read a proclamation and Archer M. Bowles, head of Fox's Northern California Division officially gave the dedicatory speech. By 9:00 p.m. the audience enthusiastically welcomed the visiting celebrities: El Brendel, the famous Swedish impersonator and vaudeville, radio and film star Irish actress Maureen O'Sullivan; radio singer Maurice Gunsky, and singing comedienne Marjorie White (White later became famous as Jane in the Tarzan movies). These three stars did a comical skit. The celebrities were present at the ten o'clock showing and also were presented to the outdoor audience at Hunter Plaza.

Meanwhile the crowd at Hunter Plaza grew to over twenty thousand. Aside from the performances by the local Karl Ross drill team, the Karl Ross glee club and Optimist Club's quartet, a thirty-piece band, led by Charles D. Smith, played in between vaudeville acts and

later for the dance. Fanchon and Marcos, a well-known vaudeville entertainment booking company, brought in several acts from San Francisco and the Bay Area. Among them were Gunsky, the Three Dynamos balancing act, a black song and dance act, comical monkeys and bears, an acrobatic team, and an accordionist and singer.

On October 15, 1930, both local papers filed full reports of the grand opening. According to the *Stockton Daily Independent*, "Thousands found the theater to be even more beautiful than advance description." Three separate writers wrote from various awe-struck points of view, one calling the new theater a "Magic Fairy Palace." Another said "the new theater is a beautiful mounted sparkling jewel of entertainment." Yet another said, "It is the last word in architectural splendor, drawing those entering the theater into a world apart…a return to the days of the Dons when cool recesses and full arcades made a repose of time for meditation. Here patrons will relax in luxury that is reminiscent of a king's court while the magic silver screen will dart images of beauty depicting romance, love and happiness." It is quite easy to comprehend the exuberance and awe that fell upon the audience when they finally had a chance to see the interior of the grand theater. Most people were actually caught by surprise that something so grand had come to be in Stockton.

The formula for the success of the Fox lay mostly with men of vision, a great civic and community partnership, and the committed leadership within the Fox Northern California Division. William Fox headed the original Fox West Coast Theater Corporation until the Stock Market Crash of 1929 and he went bankrupt. It was others in the organization who in spite of the company's internal turmoil kept it going. Foremost to support the Stockton cause were Winfield Sheehan, Charles M. Thall, Frank Whitbeck, Robert Harvey, A. M. Bowles and, most importantly, Nicholas O. Turner. Sheehan had gone from general sales manager for the company to vice president and general manager and president by 1914. He actually ran the company and built it into a strong corporation. Charles Thall was the booker-deluxe choosing films according to the type of theaters and the characteristics of the cities and the people's interest. Frank Whitbeck served as the publicity director for the entire Fox West Coast chain. He previewed all the films and wrote articles for ways to promote upcoming features. Whitbeck worked in close relationship with Robert Harvey, the company's publicity manager. A. M. Bowles headed the Northern and Central California Division. While stationed in San Francisco, he selected movies that not only entertained the locals but were also intended to attract out-of-town visitors, thus, making the theater a magnet entertainment center.

Without a doubt, Nicholas O. Turner, also known as Nick, played the largest role in making the entire operation a success. Turner arrived in Stockton eight years earlier when Fox signed its lease with the Wilhoit family. He was responsible for building up the theater's patronage. Legend had it that when he arrived and saw the T & D, he remarked that the lights in front were unattractive and the response was "they were good enough for this town." But Nick did not accept that attitude and he set to work to not only beautify the theater, but also to bring in the best pictures and to book the best road shows. Soon the T & D ranked as the strongest within the Fox circuit. Turner was still not satisfied and sought to build a better theater. An immensely popular man he was literally in the thick of the community spirit. Friends questioned why Turner came to Stockton when he could be in any city in America. In response, Turner replied, "Get away from Stockton for a while, compare it with other places and you will know what we have here. The people here are nice. Stockton has a future such as few towns have." George Rosch brought in by Fox management to direct the publicity for the opening said, "To hear Nick talk, you'd think Stockton is the biggest town in California."

For his efforts Turner received a large bonus which he used for a trip around the world. Upon his return, he faced several new challenges – that of selling the theater and all that it could be to Stocktonians and her nearby communities. In addition Turner was well aware that the public had less expendable income and that the theater's complex financing structure required stringent financial obligations that needed to be met. Very quickly the theater manager became very creative as a businessman.

Sylvia Sun Minnick

Memories

Main Street in the 1930s was really the DOWNTOWN of Stockton and had a thriving business district. All the street cars routed directly to downtown. Lots of people believed Stockton was important because it rated a place like this [the FOX]. It was located near the courthouse and, I believe, the "powers-to-be" set out to make it the best of the best for location and public events.
    — Jim Yost

I went to the T&D in 1914 when my aunt took me to see Anna Pavolva. When Pavolva seemingly floated out my immediate thought was "Wow!" I also saw John Philip Sousa at the T&D in 1921.
    — Dean De Carli

My former mother-in-law, Jeanette Rose Mack, was an organist at the T&D theater.
    — Erma De Carli

In 1926 I cut school and went to the matinee performance of the operetta Student Prince with the original Broadway cast at the Fox. It was beautifully done and it was the first time I had ever heard of the town of Heidelberg. The next day I was called into the Dean's Office to explain my absence.
    — Dolores Rimassa Belew

In 1930 I was eight years old and the Fox was opened. I went with my brothers to the Rialto, Sierra and the Fox. It was only five cents.
    — Alex Spanos

Chapter 4
The Community Centre

The outlook at the beginning of the 1930s seemed grim nationally with the onset of the market crash and the rolling effects of the Great Depression marching westward. Stockton's reaction was less severe for the city was cushioned by an enthusiasm for growth which began in the mid-1920s. As the downtown's public and private buildings changed the skyline, so too did the leaders of the community focus on other improvements. In 1925 the citizens of Stockton heartily endorsed a $1,307,000 Deep Water Bond, the voting ratio a whopping thirteen to one. President Calvin Coolidge signed a bill supporting this project two years later. The channel's widening to a depth of thirty-two feet began in 1928; this made the old steamboat routes accessible to ships from around the world. The town also moved goods and people through her

Bank of Stockton Archives

MAIN STREET, Circa 1959

three major rail companies: Santa Fe, Southern Pacific and Western Pacific. Major roads and highways quickly followed when the State Division of Highways established a district office to design and plan highways in San Joaquin and ten surrounding counties. Clearly, Stocktonians knew their assets lay in agriculture and transportation.

Stockton had many financial obligations at stake and many projects in the works regardless of the national mood. But there was something new and exciting that gave respite – the Fox California Theatre. Local native Jim Yost indicated, "Lots of people believed Stockton was important because it rated a place like this [the Fox]. It was located near the courthouse on Main Street. All the street cars routed directly to Main Street. And Main Street in the 1930s was really *the downtown* of Stockton."

Local Fox manager Nick Turner knew that while money was tight he needed to increase the attendance

numbers from the old T & D days and sustain a level of continued patronage. Being well liked by the press and in good standing with business leaders and city hall, Turner knew he had enough support to meet the bond obligations and do right by the investors as well as the Fox Corporation, to ensure that they receive a steady return for their investment. Many who bought the bonds were local citizens, albeit the more wealthy ones.

It was Turner's vision to make the Fox a community center, a place to socialize, to see and be seen, to escape into the fantasy that Hollywood provided, and to luxuriate in the comforts of the theater's – thick carpets, plush seats, and air conditioning, in essence an ethereal experience. Besides films and stage shows the theater also could serve as a setting for amateur shows and had enough available space for local organizations to hold

Crockery or even the carnival glassware, shown above, was given as bonuses for attending on dish/ China nights.

meetings. The theater and the latest films would be perfect for charities to use for fundraising purposes. All that Nick Turner envisioned became a reality.

Turner knew how to whet the moviegoers' appetite. He encouraged the newspapers to review the latest

This was the first major production filmed on the African continent. The admission price was $1 and $1.50.

movies. The Fox took out advertisements and quite often as many as two or three graphics appeared in the same daily. When the movie had a special feature. such as that of the May 1931 film *Trader Horn*, the first ever filmed on location in the heart of Africa, photos as well as the review filled several news columns.

For the price of admission, one was afforded a feature movie, travelogue, newsreel, cartoons and, frequently, stage shows put on by visiting troupes. As further enticement it offered various prizes or giveaways on different nights that drew record crowds. The most

This sample cookbook was also a giveaway in 1936. Recipes were purportedly submitted by movie stars. The booklet also included tips on makeup and fashions.

Jerry Sola Collection

popular was on *China Night* when an admission ticket also included free dishes, glass plates, carnival ware or some type of crockery. Families collected complete sets or traded among themselves to augment missing pieces. Even special cookbooks became collectors' items. Advertisements often specified the night's bonuses. By the Forties amateur nights gave away pen sets, radios, nylons and even butter. Obviously, the Fox gave their clients more than a fair return for their continued patronage; some of these items were hard to get particularly during the Depression and War.

San Joaquin County Historical Museum

Typical Dish/China Night at the Fox where hundreds of women went to the theater for an evening of entertainment.

Courtesy of Margaret Van Vranken Ficovich

VICTORY SCHOOL-Second Grade 1932
Many of these youngsters, like other school children, became members of the Mickey Mouse Club.

ESPECIALLY FOR THE CHILDREN

Turner wanted the Fox to be a place for all members of the family and children were no exception. Two short months after the grand opening was the Christmas season and Christmas belongs to children. This was a perfect time for the Fox to play to the younger set. The Fox staff came up with ideas and put their plan into operation – a Christmas show with gifts and prizes. They announced a special free Christmas show exclusively for the children set for December 22, 1930. The *Stockton Daily Evening Record* willingly co-sponsored the event and gave the upcoming event good coverage.

Nick Turner, dubbed "St. Nick" for the occasion, underestimated the power of advertisement. On that cold December 22, 1930, morning at about 7:00 a.m. children began to line up in front of the theater for the 9:00 a.m. door opening. The children were shivering; so Turner ordered the doors opened. By 8:00 a.m. the theater was filled. The staff began to search out the single seats and they were immediately taken. With the help of a police officer and also personnel from the fire department, Turner received permission to allow two children to occupy one seat. The announcer then asked that smaller children sit on the laps of the older children "…to be sure, some of them were snuggled three to a seat, but the party was all the jollier" reported the press. An estimated 6,000 children crammed into the seats, the orchestra pit, sat on the edge of the stage and in every inch of space possible including those squeezed into the lobby even though they were unable to view the movies. The remaining two or three hundred still standing on the sidewalk were totally disappointed for while they received toys they were told they had arrived too late and were turned away.

Originally there were 3,000 toys available and upon seeing the size of the incoming crowd Turner ordered another 3,000 and that was still not enough. In total Fox purchased a total of 10,000 toys. Members of the American Legion's women's auxiliary and the *Stockton Record* staff handed out two to three toys per child choosing playthings that best suited the child. Considering the vast number in attendance, the staff at the end concluded that the children were well behaved.

The Christmas show was an instant hit; it was followed by Saturday matinees whereby parents could drop their children off and knew they would be safe and have fun. The admission was only ten cents even for the adults accompanying a child. Many downtown merchants and the local newspapers alternated co-sponsoring the matinees. Quite often the sponsoring merchant helped augment the admission fare and had children bring in soda bottle caps or present special passes schools received from the downtown businesses. Children who volunteered for traffic patrol got free admission as a bonus.

In the early Fall of 1931 Eleanor Meadows, hired to run special programs at the Fox, visited the city's grammar schools seeing mostly the third to sixth grade classes. She told of a new Fox statewide concept, a Mickey Mouse Club. This children's program

What Is It?

Watch Sunday's Independent
PARENTS WATCH
BOYS AND GIRLS WATCH

ED VAN VRANKEN – 1930 was an officer of the Mickey Mouse Club.

as an officer of the newly-formed club. Young nine-year old Edward Van Vranken, a student at Victory School, was told to get on stage along with the other students. They were to "look important" even though there were no duties assigned to the position. Besides the master of ceremonies and song leaders, there were about ten club officers and a Chief Mickey Mouse and a Chief Minnie Mouse. Once, as a special treat, Mrs. Meadows took the officers down to Fresno so they could see and be a part of the Mickey Mouse Club there.

The press gave the upcoming Mickey Mouse Club plenty of coverage and ran an official membership application form that was accepted at the box office as well as at the newspaper office. The first meeting, held October 17, 1931, during the first anniversary week of the Fox, drew fifteen hundred children according to the *Stockton Daily Independent*. The following week, with increased promotion, that membership number reached several thousand. Even youth as old as fifteen years of age belonged to the Mickey Mouse Club. Many influential people from the national and local level received honorary membership status: President Herbert Hoover, Governor Rolph, Mayor Tremain, Eugene Wilhoit, Councilmen Wheeler, Richards, Pengelly and Oneto. The honorary membership also included City Manager Walter

would be chocked full of activities such as movies, cartoons, local talent shows and plenty of prizes. The idea caught on and Mrs. Meadows received hearty endorsements from the schools and teachers. She then looked for a representative from each school to serve

Hogan, City Superintendent of Schools Ansel S. Williams, County Superintendent of Schools John R. Williams, and General Otto Sandman. Statewide, the Fox organization boasted a membership of 750,000.

As a member of the Mickey Mouse Club, the child received a membership card and a Mickey Mouse Club button. At the theater, the doors opened at 9 o'clock and by 9:45 a.m. the program was underway. The theater organ was used as a guide to hold the youngsters' attention and for singalongs. The program began with an oath, a creed, theme songs, a yell, movies, cartoons, and talent shows featuring local dance studios and youth groups. If a child who could sing, dance or even play a harmonica, he was encouraged to enter the weekly talent contest. Parents saw the rewards of

Courtesy of Evelyn Coldani Cintola

MICKEY MOUSE CLUB TO FETE BIRTHDAY

Local dance group entertains at a Saturday matinee.

– 35 –

providing their children with music lessons. When the children exited, the sponsoring merchant gave out token prizes.

Clearly, as defined by the following Mickey Mouse creed, the intent of the Mickey Mouse Club was two fold: to provide clean entertainment and to promote good citizenship:

I will be a square shooter in my home, in school, on the playgrounds, wherever I may be.

I will be truthful and honorable and strive always to make myself a better and more useful little citizen.

I will respect my elders, help the aged, the helpless and children smaller than myself.

In short, I will be a good American.

Even though Nick Turner and his wife were childless, he was devoted to the well being of children. During Saturday matinees, as the line of children

---

wrapped around the outside of the theater on down San Joaquin Street, Turner patrolled the entire route checking on the youngsters' safety. If a child gifted Nick Turner with a drawing or some small token, he happily displayed it in his office during his tenure in Stockton.

By the start of World War II the Mickey Mouse Club no longer issued membership cards. While attendance remained high, the staff could no longer control the rowdy; so the program activities came to a halt. Merchants continued to provide small giveaways and the theater showed serials, a feature movie, cartoons and newsreels. This change did not spell a decline for the hundreds who attended the Saturday matinee; children and their parents continued to be Fox California's devotees.

THE FIRST ANNIVERSARY

Beginning on October 11, 1931, the Fox California set off a spectacular week-long celebration to commemorate its first anniversary. Some people even speculated that the theater entertained almost a million people during the first year of business and the theater looked ahead to even better years. The celebratory activities came in two phases, each ran for four days with complete

This advertisement for the first anniversary of the Fox California included the world premiere of the movie *Cisco Kid*.

OFFICIAL MICKEY MOUSE PROGRAM

Doors open - 9 o'clock
Master of Ceremonies – Hal Burmeister
Organ Recital – Mrs. Inez McNeil
Community Singing
Mickey Mouse Ceremonies - conducted by Club Officers
Allegiance to the Flag
Singing of "America"
Mickey Mouse Yell
Mickey Mouse Creed
Mickey Mouse Theme Song
Laurel & Hardy Comedy, "*Be Big*"
Galloping Ghosts – serial
Mickey Mouse Orchestra –
    organized by Charles D. Smith
Novelty Clog Dance – Zelda Ratto & Doris Merz
Popular Songs – Dorothy Diven
Valse Golden – dance by
    Fumi Iwata, Tashiko Iwata, Sumiko
    Tsukahara and Yoko Tsukahara
Vagabonds – dance by
    Dorothy Tucker & Jesslyn Pearson
Whistling – Tiny Roberts
La Sevilla – dance by Harriet Budlin, Aileen Bolter,
    Alice Marlette, Lucille McGeorge & Maud Myer
Pianologue – Bobbin Gay Peck
Harmonica Contest – Albert Berry, Marlon Storey,
    Elmer Wolf, Clyde Andrews, & Loring Gage
Mickey Mouse Cartoon
Adjournment until next Saturday
          Stockton Daily Independent
          October 24, 1931

A typical Saturday Mickey Mouse Program utilizing local talent and dance groups.

changes in movies and programs. The first four nights' feature was a coup for Stockton's Fox for it hosted the world premiere of the *Cisco Kid*, a movie directed by Raoul Walsh and filmed in Tucson. It starred Warner Baxter with Conchita Montenegro as his leading lady. For four days the movie, along with the usual cartoons and newsreel, ran nine times daily with the last showing at 10:30 p.m. A live portion of the evening program included a Fanchon and Marcos' "Idea" Parasol Anniversary Revue; the Sunkist Beauties, a spectacular bicycle whirlwind act featuring twelve unicyclists performing a ballet; a number of vaudeville entertainers and, curiously, Captain Willie Mauss known to have taught Baron von Richtofen (the Red Baron) to fly. The local orchestra played in between the acts.

The second four nights showing featured MGM's *Sidewalks of New York* starring Buster Keaton with Cliff Edwards and Anita Page. Irish tenor Don Smith, serving as the master of ceremonies, introduced the live portion of the program that included Peggy O'Neill's peppy Merrymakers, the Four Covans described as red-hot hoofers, Nelson & Knight, a comedy sailor act, and the Sweet Sixteen Sweethearts called the liveliest group of girls. Every night the theater filled to capacity and every minute was packed with action.

On the anniversary date, October 14th local bakery owner Otto Gern presented a large three-tier birthday cake to the theater. The *Stockton Independent* on October 15th even listed the ingredients used by bakers

A song sheet from Fanchon & Marco's *Ideas* show. The Fox's first anniversary week's program included a Franchon and Marco stage production. Fanchon (Fanny) Wolff and Mike (Marco) Wolff were a brother-sister ballroom dance team of the 1920s-30s. They turned promoters-producers of stage shows and had five separate groups of dancers that rotated between Los Angeles and Vancouver, BC.

Con Donis and Clarence Leightner: ten dozen eggs, two gallons of milk, twenty pounds of sugar, twenty pounds of flour and ten pounds of butter all of which was blended in an eighty quart mixing bowl. Compliments abounded for the theater by civic organizations and citizens. The

Downtown Association was cited as its main booster. Like a love fest, the theater received an equal amount of similar sentiments. Much of the accolades occurred at a luncheon given by the Downtown Association at the Stockton Country Club to honor Nick Turner and Fox's Northern and Central Division head A.M. Bowles. Fox, in turn, presented banker Eugene Wilhoit with a golden pass to all the Fox West Coast theaters citing Wilhoit's significant role in making the Fox California a reality.

The Fox adapted readily to changing conditions. In 1933 the governor of California declared a bank holiday and in the same week President

May 1932, one admission ticket provided patrons with three different forms of entertainment: a movie, live musical review and an industrial show.

Jerry Sola Collection

The rotunda area shows the fountain filled with fish. In the 1930s, the biggest giveaways on Bank Nights had drawings of cash which was as much as $750 to $1,000.

Franklin D. Roosevelt issued a nationwide bank holiday. With the banks closed and a cash shortage, Fox management announced they were willing to accept checks in lieu of cash. A check needed to include one's name, address and the exact amount of the admission fee. The notice went on to say, "…the management has full confidence in the integrity and stability of the people in the present emergency." By simply offering another method of monetary exchange, the people's ability to still escape into the dreams created by Hollywood never ceased.

It was shortly after the first anniversary of the Fox California that Nick Turner sold his house in the 1200 block of West Willow Street and moved into the Eden Square Apartments on North El Dorado Street facing Eden Park. There the Turners remained until 1934 when they moved to San Francisco following his promotion to head the Northern and California Division of the Fox West Coast organization. Nick Turner spent a little over a decade in Stockton. It was Stockton's loss but Fox leadership recognized they had an employee with vision and talent.

Many years later Stocktonian Ed Van Vranken, a former Mickey Mouse member and neighbor of Turner, ran into Nick in San Francisco. After a bit of reminiscing about the years he spent in Stockton, Turner admitted he suffered great trepidation every

time he signed work contracts and receipts for construction and materials costs. He had never built a theater before much less realize the horrendous cost involved. As to living in Stockton and operating the theater, Turner had only glowing memories.

Ray Duddy replaced Turner and he, too, quickly endeared himself to the community. Many of the activities that Turner started continued under Duddy's watch: hundreds of children were faithful to the Saturday matinees, the Fox continued to advertise heavily in the press, movies received rave reviews, giveaways drew record attendance, and there were occasional visiting stage shows or headlining personalities. Duddy also introduced new ways to market the Fox. Whenever a manufacturing company or even a local merchant wanted to exhibit, literally, from soup to nuts, and in some cases from refrigerators to clothing, space at the Fox was accessible. Industrial shows drew the crowd to the products lining the east lobby wall. Quite often the Chamber of Commerce held raffle drawings with the prize being a late model car parked in front of the theater.

Contests and amateur hours became popular. People flocked to the Fox on Election Night in 1940 to find out the latest results, particularly when the nation was re-electing Franklin D. Roosevelt to his third term. KWG broadcast the election news from the

Courtesy of Haggin Museum

Courtesy of Jill Bennett Heard

INDUSTRIAL AND LOCAL DISPLAYS ON THE EAST WALL OF THE THEATER LOBBY

Refrigerators shown came from O.L. Mallet, Eddy Electric and Mechanical Company and Con J. Franke, electrical contractor (and City Councilman), among others. The price of the Frigidaire, sixth unit from the left, was $87.40. The Shirley Temple doll atop the fourth unit from the left is significant because the revenue from Temple's very popular 1930s movies helped make 20th Century Fox a major film studio. Local tailor, Nick Pomponio, had his business on the corner of Sutter and Main Streets for many years. He used the Fox lobby to great advantage by promoting his men's suits there.

lobby and while it was easy to keep tab of the results via home radios, just being down at the Fox made one feel energized by all the tension. Radio station KSFO also transmitted from the California Fox. On Saturdays at midnight, entertainer Rolly Langley conducted a lively "Party Time" whereby the audience participated in the radio broadcast. There were plenty of prizes and many people formed their own groups. The midnight show also included the feature movie making it a long night. Downtown's Main Street buzzed into the wee hours of the morning.

The Fox played an important role throughout the World War II years. Here the crowds rushed to see the latest Fox newsreels telling of activities on the war front. Many felt their patriotism building within their veins as Hollywood pumped out a variety of war and war-related movies. The War Department used exhibits, loud speakers mounted on buses, photo displays and nearly everything possible to promote the sale of war bonds. Often times these exhibits were coordinated with a particular feature movie. For instance in 1942 with the feature movie *Flying Tigers* starring John Wayne, the War Department parked a long truck in front of the theater. On it sat a Japanese two-man submarine, the interior clearly visible through portholes drilled through its side. The submarine, captured off the coast of Barbour's Point, Honolulu on December 8, 1941, was part of a seven-submarine flotilla of minisubs whose mission was to infiltrate Honolulu's Pearl Harbor.

This was the only one captured. A truck hauled the submarine around the country and inspired tremendous patriotic sentiments and a successful war bond drive. In another war-time display, but a bit more humorous, someone tethered a white horse outside the Fox, stating it belonged to Emperor Hirohito. It seemed plausible as the emperor was often photographed on a white horse. The comment made later was that the horse probably belonged to someone in Farmington. Nevertheless, the horse and the Fox served an important purpose.

During the war years, fundraisers and displays brought out the crowd; it was a chance for one to be patriotic and be entertained. Both Edison High and Stockton High's students were granted one period off to attend the war bond rallies held at the Fox. Some remembered them as "very spirited" affairs. Nightly, before a show began, an announcer stirred up the folks and encouraged them to buy bonds or donate to the cause, setting a reasonable amount that could be raised, perhaps, two hundred dollars for the evening. During intermission young people took up the collection as they made their way down the aisles row by row with their collection trays. Others manned tables in the lobby ready to sell bonds. At the end of the evening the audience had a good idea how much was collected. Beauty contests were yet another way to raise money. Winning depended on the number of tickets contestants sold or the amount they or their family raised for the charity. Appearances and talent were not major factors.

Courtesy of the Haggin Museum

Courtesy of the Haggin Museum

The War Bond display bus captured the crowd. *Little Tokyo, U.S.A.*, a 1942 Fox spy drama starring Preston Foster, was one of the movies playing at the time.

Jerry Sola Collection

On display is the Japanese Midget Sub HA-19 captured December 8, 1941, off the coast of Oahu, Hawaii. It was completely dismantled, examined by the Navy, reassembled with portholes installed for viewing, mounted on a trailer and exhibited on a U.S tour. The movie showing was *Flying Tigers* starring John Wayne in his first war film.

Courtesy of Haggin Museum

1945 Fox volunteers collecting for the war effort. Left to Right: Bessie Pappas, Erma Viviano Gianelli, Dorothy Trachiotis Henning, Lily Wong Chin, Evelyn Mar Pong, Katherine Huntalas Skandale, unidentified, Helen Ng, Thea Besotes and Lucky Toy.

Jerry Sola Collection

Haggin Museum

Left: War bonds sold in the lobby during intermission. Right: A plaque placed in the lobby to honor the 220 members of the Fox West Coast Theaters' staff serving in the military during World War II.

AFTER THE WAR

In the decades of the late 1940s and into the 1950s, Saturday matinees continued to be popular with children's admission still a dime or a Pepsi bottle cap or two milk caps depending on the sponsoring local merchant. Merchants also continued to provide token giveaways such as pencils, erasers or small useful items and a piece of candy when they exited the theater. Happyholmes Dairy sponsored a number of these Saturday matinees, the admission a cap from a milk bottle. There were generally two movies or serials, such as westerns with Hopalong Cassidy or Roy Rogers or the

Courtesy of Jill Bennett Heard

The band is performing for the Fifth War Bond Drive of 1944.

Courtesy of Haggin Museum

People flocked to the Fox for the movies and to keep abreast of the latest news on the war. The theater served as a community center at a time when the nation felt great unrest.

EDDIE LE BARON often appeared at the Saturday matinees as a local idol to inspire the youngsters. He promoted good citizenship and healthy living.

battles between space traveler Flash Gordon and the diabolic Emperor Ming. Cartoons and Fox Movietone Newsreel preceded inspiration talks by guest speakers such as hometown football hero Eddie Le Baron and Frankie Albert, the 49er quarterback. Dean De Carli, co-owner of Happyholmes and assigned

The Dumbo display hung on the second floor north wall near the Ladies' Lounge.

to introduce the guests, reminisced that "There was generally a full audience and the children enjoyed not only the westerns but also listened attentively when famous athletes spoke of clean living, exercising and against smoking." The athletes and other celebrities' pep talks focused on good behavior or high morals.

With hundreds of children in the theater, noise and mischief often went hand in hand. On Saturday afternoons teenagers dominated the theater. Most could only afford the cheap balcony seats, but the challenge was to sneak down to the loge section without being caught by the usherettes. Another antic was to have one person buy an admission ticket and then wait until the theater staff were elsewhere and open the

side exit doors to San Joaquin Street so their friends could sneak in. A loud clanging sound as the heavy metal door closed foretold of the ruse. Often those who snuck in were not caught because of the dimness of the theater. Some of the younger set ran from one seat to another. Other pranks included throwing items down from the balcony to the floor below such as teepee. These rowdy pre-teens and teenagers created enough trouble that management augmented its staff with private patrol officers.

For three decades the Fox was a meeting point for teenagers. Those without wheels relied on their parents to drop them off to meet friends at a designated time or for a particular movie. Others fortunate enough to own a car cruised down Main Street, slowing up in front of the theater and then circling the block to begin the process all over again, all the while looking and being looked at by those in front of the theater and others hanging around Hunter Plaza. Some even remember when the principal of St. Mary's High School stood outside the Fox to make sure its students adhered to the school's ban on certain movies the administration thought would corrupt morals. One movie in particular was the 1957 movie *And God Created Woman*, starring Brigette Bardot.

A candy counter on the east wall of the lobby replaced the industrial display area. By the 1950s the counter was relocated under the grand staircase. It was a big deal to get all dressed up and take a gal to the Fox, treat her to a licorice whip, a bar of chewy *Big Hunk*, a

Teens checking out the refreshment stand in the lobby. Circa 1956

box of *Good & Plenty* or share a box of popcorn. With evening admission about twenty-five to thirty-five cents plus popcorn, one spent a whole dollar – quite a bit of money for entertainment in those days. To many the Fox was the place of their first date and even their first kiss up in the dark recess of the upper balcony.

Families flocked to the Fox for good evening entertainment. With children under tow, a night out included dinner on Main Street at Joe De Bono's for a hamburger and a shake. The Fox provided hours of entertainment, definitely something for everyone. Specific giveaway nights drew the largest audiences as did special appearances by Al Jolson, the Marx Brothers or the big bands of Paul Whitman, Ted Lewis, Duke Ellington and the "Dorseys" among others. These visiting celebrities showed that Stockton was an important city and the public was receiving top notch entertainment.

The Fox California had forty years of sustainability, but by the 1960s interest waned, lifestyles changed, and the Fox California attendance experienced a marked decline. The city limits expanded northward

The Stockton Theater on Pacific Avenue, built in 1945, was a major factor in the decline of the Fox Theatre as the population preferred to live and frequent businesses north of downtown. Circa 1959

Bank of Stockton Archives

Jill Bennett Heard

Several motor movies sprouted in the outer city limits beginning in 1949. This particular drive-in was at the 99 Speedway on Wilson Way.

"...and on the organ George Wright"

George Wright was born in Orland, California in 1920, but spent his childhood in Stockton. He learned piano at an early age, and in 1934 convinced Stockton's most noted organist, Inez McNeil, to give him lessons on the Fox Theatre's Wurlitzer-Morton. Mrs. Mac, as George called her, worked with him three hours every Sunday morning at the Fox, charging one dollar per lesson.

Sacramento's new Grant High School was blessed with an organ and wanted a student to be its organist. They recruited Wright, much as colleges recruited star athletes, offering pay and the opportunity to play all he wanted. He took the offer and left home to complete high school in Sacramento.

Courtesy of Elizabeth Steele

After high school, Wright found work at an Oakland night club and playing for a local radio station. He moved from Oakland to KFRC and later KPO (now KNBR), in San Francisco. NBC brought him to New York for more radio work. He finally became the house organist for the Paramount Theatre in New York, a rare opportunity.

Old time radio listeners will remember the days when every radio station had an organist on staff to provide themes, interludes, and entertainment. The radio "soaps" all were enhanced by organ themes and mood music. Credits at the end of a program all seemed to conclude with "...and George Wright at the Organ." This is how most became familiar with his work. In later years he was remembered as the organist for the popular TV soap *General Hospital* before it opted for recorded orchestra music.

History will remember Wright for his concerts, recitals and recordings on monster organs where he demonstrated his love of the "rumbles, roars, and shrieks" possible only on one of the surviving dinosaurs. He was the master of music's most complex instrument. It is ironic that the greatest theater organist, who matured too late for the golden age of his instrument, is credited with saving it from oblivion. And it is fitting that he was a product of Stockton and the Fox Theatre.

creating new neighborhoods and larger shopping areas; downtown was no longer the heart of the community. Although buses still ran to downtown, the transit system became inadequate as it did not link up to all parts of the city, particularly to some residential areas. The crowds used to escape the hot summer months in the coolness of the theater, but families now had that same comfort when they installed home air conditioning units. Entertainers, who once graced the stage, were now on television. The old Mickey Mouse Club came alive again but this time it did not employ local talent nor give away small prizes. It was on television and the children idolized a cast of young stars. Television eliminated the camaraderie of a city's community, but it allowed viewers to vicariously be a part of the greater universe.

The new Stockton Theater on Pacific Avenue, very much a neighborhood theater on the Miracle Mile, began to compete very successfully and cut deep into the Fox's patronage. Without attendance and with an aging theater, funds were simply not available for maintenance; the Grand Lady began to show deterioration. By the 1960s the Fox California struggled to survive. A decade and a half later the owners of the Stockton Theater bought the lease to the Fox and even the land ownership changed hands. The Fox would not regain her glamorous state until the following century. Yet from the moment of her inauguration, she was *the* first-run movie house and her generations of followers thoroughly enjoyed hours upon hours of Hollywood's fantasy.

Sylvia Sun Minnick

Memories

Main Street in the 1930s was really the DOWNTOWN of Stockton and had a thriving business district. All the street cars routed directly to downtown. Lots of people believed Stockton was important because it rated a place like this [the FOX]. It was located near the courthouse and, I believe, the "powers-to-be" set out to make it the best of the best for location and public events.
  — Jim Yost

I was seven-years-old and a student of dancing teacher Betty Hackett. We did a tap-dance routine in 1932 to entertain the kids. I also attended the movies with an older sister and our parents. A major attraction at the theater was the pond in the lobby with live fish.
  — Carolyn Eproson Mortensen

My father had hearing difficulties and always took the aisle seat whereupon he plugged in the earphones. The Fox often gave bonuses, such as crockery, for those attending. In front of the theater there were often cars displayed for raffle purposes and most of the time it was the Chamber of Commerce that sponsored these events. Lots of clubs held meetings and local events at the Fox with lots of families participating.
  — Jim Yost

My family always sat on the left side down where the slope began near the back of the theater. I liked to sit at the end of the aisle because my father bought lifesavers which would last through the whole showing and I used the white lights to identify the flavor of the candy. Sometimes I even rolled down the incline.
  — Del McComb

In 1935 the Sunday matinee at the Fox California, the best theater in town, and the hot-dog stand nearby provided the "best and cheapest date." Admission was around 25 cents and, if you got there before 5 o'clock you could get a hot dog for 10 cents.
  — Florence Strecker Allen

I would catch a streetcar at the corner of Pershing and Willow Streets and it would put me right downtown near the theater. My most vivid memory was that Alta Edwards Kopp and I went to see Gone With The Wind *and after the movies we headed home on the streetcar when Alta's boyfriend, Leo Kopp, and his friend, Irving DePauli, came by in Leo's red roadster. We got off the streetcar and joined the boys – whom we would later marry.*
  — Gladys Adams DePauli

My girlfriends and I took a streetcar to Owl Drug at California and Main Streets for lunch and then to the show. It was like Hollywood coming to Stockton. It was a grand place and no other building had as much presence. I looked forward to Saturdays. But, I think the adults got more out of the Fox than the kids.
  — Margaret Van Vranken Ficovich

My sister, Shirley, won a beauty contest at the Fox. The contest was to raise money for charity. To push for support for Shirley who was the lead contender, I asked my cousin Mike Barkett to pledge a sum and Shirley won. This was in 1943.
  — Marian Jacobs

Our young people's group attended services at St. Basil Greek Orthodox Church and we remembered Alex Spanos would give us goodies from his father's nearby restaurant so that we could have a little snack in the show.
    — *Dorothy Trachiotis Henning*

In 1944 I spied a young man descending the elegant staircase at the Fox. Several weeks later we were introduced at his request. The attraction must have been mutual for one and a half years later he became my first husband.
    — *Yvonne DuBois Hill*

The Fox Saturday matinees provided great incentives by giving free admission for those who served on the traffic patrol.
    — *Clarence Louie*

I was five-years-old in 1948 and my father got me to work for my allowance of fifty cents a week by cleaning the gum off of all the seats. I remembered I got my first kiss in the balcony at the age of sixteen in 1959.
    — *Doug Wilhoit, Jr.*

In the 1940s Edna and I attended many of the road shows including Ted Lewis and his Rhythm Rhapsody Review. The orchestra and the music were good. Duke Ellington got sick after one performance and had to cancel the other show scheduled for later in the evening.
    — *Dean De Carli*

During Saturday matinees youngsters preferred to sit in the balcony so that they could throw items down to the lower level such as toilet paper. These pranks were more like jokes compared to today's standards.
    — *Gail Weldy Traverso*

As a kid, I thought the Fox was an "incredible wonderland." Once entered it transported people into another world. The rugs had golden stars in the pattern and the pillars in the lobby reminded me of those columns in the days of Samson for they soared to great heights. The mirrors reflected the lights …and the red and green lights on the sides of the aisles and exits. The second floor had cushy rugs and when I looked over at the box seats I wondered if one day I would get to sit there.
    — *Mike Fitzgerald*

Chapter 5
The Men and Women of the Fox

From the mid-1920s to the mid-1950s the Fox California West Coast Theaters were an influential force. Their movies served as respite from the hardships of the Depression and World War II. Going to the movies was the reward for people who toiled at their labor, and a good story was the vehicle to escape some of the harsh realities of life. Movies touched the gamut of human emotions – happiness, sadness, even pathos. When one remembers a particular movie he will frequently also recall where it was shown and even the ambiance of the times. No surroundings or comfort zone just happens; it is created, planned and executed by the many men and women behind the production and by the number of people who run the movie house from the top echelon to the local managers and even to that part-timer teenager working behind the candy counter.

William Fox was the first great mogul of the movie business. He made movies and owned or controlled the theaters where they played. Like Broadway showmen Florenz Ziegfeld and S. L. Roxy, he named his theaters after himself. It not only fed his ego, it looked very good on a theater marquee. By 1930 the entertainment octopus he created was in trouble on several fronts. The cost of adding sound equipment to movie houses he owned or controlled, the loss of attendance due to the Great Depression, and anti-trust suits put Fox into bankruptcy. He

> *"Those who worked for Turner realized that jobs were scarce during the Depression and getting a job at the Fox meant good pay and an opportunity of a lifetime."*

tried to reassure a protective committee of Class A stockholders that his assets exceeded liabilities. But, like many other major corporate leaders he did face financial ruin. In 1935, Fox Film Corporation merged with Darryl F. Zanuck's 20th Century Pictures and the venture became known as 20th Century Fox Film Corporation. When William Fox's bankruptcy legal proceedings ensued, he attempted to bribe a judge and was sentenced to prison. He was paroled in 1943 and attempted to set up his own production firm again but could not find backers. Fox was never able to establish his entertainment empire again.

Jerry Sola Collection

Manager Nick Turner and the usherette staff preparing Easter baskets. Circa 1932

getting a job at the Fox meant good pay and an opportunity of a lifetime.

The original staff included P. L. Misita, assistant manager; Inez McNeil, organist; James E. Cox, maintenance man; the five projectionists were Lee Allard, Tillman J. Meadows, William Thompson, Harold Landon, and Charles Bailey. Ethel Rogers and Bernice Turner were the cashiers; Tom Kay was the house artist. Eleanor Meadows, wife of the projectionist Tillman J., was hired as the program manager and coordinated local talent shows including those for the Saturday Mickey Mouse program. Mrs. Meadows became a familiar face at the various schools and worked well with the local merchants who sponsored some of the Saturday events. It was only after several years and the youngsters' becoming too raucous and showing no interest in seeing local talent that Mrs. Meadows changed the format.

READY TO SERVE

Fox's bankruptcy brought new leadership and new focus when Harley L. Clarke bought William Fox's controlling 151,000 shares of common stock for $18 million. Clarke, a millionaire utilities magnate and an engineer by profession, had a deep interest in educational films and the latest advancement in theater equipment. With this type of background Clarke was mentally equipped to analyze the 32-house theater chain's challenging times. He needed the right men to run the top divisions of the corporation, career individuals who could handle the multi-faceted duties of a manager at the local level and creative producers and directors to crank out quality movies to satisfy the public's interest. Clarke had Winfield Sheehan, Charles M. Thall, A.M. Bowles and many others at the corporate level. Others like Nicholas O. Turner handled the individual theaters in the local communities.

Early on Nick Turner knew that good management and a dedicated staff were the keys to keep Stockton's Fox California running smoothly. He was noted for Fox's high standard of entertainment and a staff with equal expectations. From the projection room to housekeeping, everyone knew to give the best possible service. Turner imbued them with pride and pleasure, something he called the Fox code of courtesy. Turner's quality of leadership was measured by the respect and affection of his workers. Those who worked for Turner realized that jobs were scarce during the Depression and

The Fox used the organ several times a week for the Saturday morning kiddie shows, during Bank Night, china giveaways and the inevitable amateur nights. Mrs. Inez McNeil, better known as Mrs. Mac by most regulars, could "entice beautiful sounds out of the original nine-rank Wurlitzer Model 210 that had been continually added to in ranks, manuals and couplers. As the world-renown organist George Wright would say, "Somehow this conglomeration of the works of various builders hung together to make beautiful sounds and Mrs. Mac certainly knew how to coax them out. If

Courtesy of Greg Meadows

ELEANOR MEADOWS was the coordinator of programs at the Fox which included the Mickey Mouse matinees and its live entertainment. Meadows worked with local merchants to sponsor many of the giveaway bonuses.

anyone deserves credit for showing me how to play a rhythm tune or put together a show medley it's dear Mrs. Mac." McNeil and her family owned the McNeil & Company Music Store on Main Street and she purportedly had Stockton's largest collection of sheet music.

Helen Hanson was the head usherette and the others who worked on rotation shifts were Juanita Anderson, Lydia Predictali, Lucille Locklin, Sarah Shuster, Eva Funk, Rose Pistichini, Beulah Gray, Hazel Snell, Betty Elliot, Virginia Pearson, Alva Starr, Bernice Bertolas, Mildred Barley, Ina Johnson, Geraldine Cooper, Pearl Rand and Verna Hill. Most were either still in high school or had just graduated. The turnover in usherettes was high, many knew it was a temporary job until either they returned to school, or got married, or were able to find other employment. By 1937 Frances Parker had become the head usherette and Betty Davidson the assistant head.

Except for the manager and assistant manager, who were known to don tuxedos on holidays and special night events, the rest of the staff that greeted the public wore uniforms. The usherette uniforms evolved through the years, often following a popular movie or a trend created by popular stars such as Marlene Dietrich. The initial outfit was ankle-length culottes, long sleeves and

Courtesy of Elizabeth Steele

ELIZABETH MCNEIL at the organ in 1930. A theater organist, McNeil played at the T & D and later at the Fox. Her family owned a music store on Main Street. She was noted for being world-renowned George Wright's teacher and mentor.

wide white lapels with white rim hats decorated with a black headband. Very shortly the uniform changed to straight pants and short jackets that flared from the waistline. In 1934 a local headline announced "Usherettes Go Lupe Velez" a Spanish theme made famous by the Latina movie star. When interviewed the usherettes indicated they liked their new attire better than the former semi-military uniforms for they felt the new outfit was more feminine given the flared culottes, white puff elbow-length sleeves and a stylish wide cummerbund. Following this style, the pants style remained the same but the top had long mutton-sleeves with satin stripes looking much like drum majorettes. In the 1950s people remembered uniforms similar to that of the Philip Morris bellhop. These uniforms became a status symbol for many of the teenage employees and the envy of their peers. Frequently a new employee worked in all three capacities of usherette, cashier and

Courtesy of Greg Massei

Fox usherette staff in dress uniforms in 1931.

Courtesy of Greg Massei

In 1932 the usherette uniform took on a semi-military flare.

about three to four hours of working the lights, sound and projectors. Consequently, the theater needed projectionists to work in shifts. According to the Society of Motion Picture and Television Engineers' (SMPTE) "Motion Picture Project and Theatre Presentation" manual there are two types, those who become bored, indifferent or discouraged about a seemingly mundane job were considered "movie machine operators," and not projectionists. A projectionist is a professional. "It is in their pride, perseverance and knowledge that the art and science of the entire motion-picture industry ultimately rests," according to the manual. Most noticeably the projectionist checks and double checks shipments of canisters, sequences of reel bands, reel tapes, sound recordings and amplification. Cleaning the projectors require several steps into many intricate parts such as lenses, rollers, pads, film tracks and so forth. Dirt, oil, traces of wax do not escape the projectionist's discernible eyes and neither does looseness or misalignment of film on the reels. The projectionist also lights the auditorium for intermission conditions and depends heavily on the cooperation of the lower floor staff to advise on the sound level and focus drift. Logging running time of each reel, recording the setting of the projector, rewinding and reporting on the condition of the film after each use as well as other special notes prior to

the candy counter person; to them, there was also a gradation in assignment with the ticket seller having the prime job, followed by the candy counter girl, and then the usherettes. Being in the ticket booth meant one could see and be seen, and behind the candy counter one could exchange greetings with the regular customers. The usherette, however, was ever ready with her flashlight to guide customers to their seats or use it to shine quickly on rowdy teens to silence them. Nick Turner and Ray Duddy drilled into the usherettes the importance of courtesy and customer service. When interviewed the usherettes indicated they were not allowed to take tips and even the girls, themselves said, "offers (for tips) take away the pleasure of doing little favors." The words "graciousness" and "courtesy" come to mind. The young doormen, mostly teenagers, had no uniform except a jacket and tie.

The entertainment often included two feature movies, news report, cartoons, preview of upcoming features and even live performances. All in all the show took

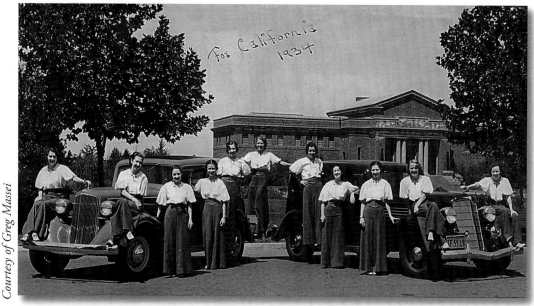

Courtesy of Greg Massei

"Usherettes Go 'Lupe Velez'" read the captions in a newspaper article in 1934. The staff modeled in front of the Haggin Museum showing off the more feminine attire in keeping with the Spanish theme made famous by Latina movie star, Lupe Velez. Among those in this photo are Velda Schott, head usherette, Ethel Best, Urida Wade, Berniece Frambolo, Claudia Morris and Frances Packard.

Courtesy of Ann Gallo Lina

These are the men and women of the Fox West Coast Theaters staff of Stockton who worked at the Fox California, the Ritz and the State in 1940. Ray Duddy, Fox manager, is near the center of the fireplace with glasses and a dark suit. Ann Lina is seated in the middle just to the right of the woman in a fur piece.

TILLMAN J. MEADOWS, one of the original five projectionists when the Fox opened in 1930. His wife was also on staff at the theater as the program coordinator.

JOE HOLT, a projectionist at the Fox, received his training at RCA in New York City. He worked at various theaters in Stockton and was also a sound and lighting man for many films made in Stockton, including Fat City. Circa 1969.

ANN GALLO LINA began working at the Fox as an usherette and within six months became the theater's bookkeeper.

Courtesy of Peggy Weldy Traverso

Supervisor Pearl Gallegos (with glasses) and Peggy Weldy on a busy night behind the candy counter in 1956.

LAVERNE BABCOOK, a 17-year old, worked at the Fox while attending Stockton Junior College. During her time there she worked as an usherette and later became a cashier. She began working at the Fox in 1941.

PEGGY WELDY TRAVERSO was only 16 when she started working at the Fox as an usherette and then at the candy counter.

sending the reels on their way to other movie houses add up to tremendous paperwork for the technician. The projectionist with the longest tenure was Charles Bailey who worked at the Fox from 1930 to 1969. Retired projectionist Joe Holt, who worked at several of the movie theaters including the Fox, remembered that the movies at the Fox lasted four days and then were shifted to the Ritz. The theory was that a movie stayed at one theater as long as there was a gross profit. In later years with the advent of televised fights, the television projectors were the size of an eighteen cubic foot refrigerator. Cables for sound came into the project room and the picture equipment was on the lower floor in the seating area about twenty-five feet from the screen.

The bookkeeper, maintenance employees and security guards were just as important even though they had less contact with the general public. One particular bookkeeper, Ann Lina (nee Gallo) started out in 1937 as an usherette and switched for a short period into the ticket booth before taking over the rein of bookkeeper, a quick six month rise in responsibility. The theater, by then, had a staff of 32 employees: manager Ray Duddy, Georgia Knight as his secretary, an assistant manager, eight usherettes, four doormen, one engineer, seven projectionists, three cashiers and six janitors headed by Margaret Sneed. Ann often worked past midnight reconciling the day's take being that the box office closed around 9:30pm.

Running a theater was particularly tough for local managers needing to balance receipts, payroll and operational costs. Admission tickets prior to the Depression ran from $2.50 for orchestra and loges, $2.00 for dress circle and $1.00 for balcony. During the Depression management charged only what traffic could bear and the price of tickets plummeted to only fifty cents with the loge section costing a dime more. A full house of kiddies on Saturday matinee at ten cents a seat brought in only $200. The daily receipts were deemed barely profitable. In the ensuing years the theater advertised special weekend and night bargains such as 500 seats at twenty-five cents each which came to only $125 and adding the regular price for the rest of the seats, the house total was less than $1,000.

Payroll cost just over one thousand dollars a week. The manager received a weekly salary of $106, his assistant $50 as did the secretary. Usherettes, working a 48-hour week, were paid $25 a week as were the three cashiers and the doormen (ticket takers) received fifty cents an hour. Projectionists were the highest paid at $2.07 per hour followed by the engineer at $1.56 an hour and the janitors were paid $1.09 an hour. Quite often the actual payroll expenditure exceeded the budgeted amount. Other than payroll, maintenance, utilities and overhead, rental of film could cost as much as four to five thousand dollars a week for two films, the main feature and the second attraction. Rental of the promotional material such as a full sheet (27"x41") half sheet (22"x28"), inserts (14"x36"), lobby cards (11"x14") and stills (8"x10") ran as high as fifty dollars a week. Even matting the studio photos for display cost as much as fourteen dollars.

The Fox West Coast organization required that each of its theaters fill out a mountain of paper work. Weekly, the theater returned to the organization five and one-quarter percent of the gross receipts plus twenty five percent of the net candy sales. In 1946, a Theatre Manager's Weekly Report required a breakdown of the attendance tickets into the loge and general admission sections as well as the number of free passes collected for both matinees and evenings. In the same report the candy sales needed to be compared to the actual inventory. The weekly check register reported on the cost of film, insurance, sales taxes, utilities, local advertising including the matting of posters and promotional material. One weekly report even showed that the theater paid $2.98 to Southern Pacific to express a supply of paper towels to the theater, $5.25 to Pioneer Transfer for moving the candy machine, and $30.00 to Ray Bailey for three days of police service. Not surprisingly, manager Ray Duddy purportedly fished the coins out of the lobby water fountain twice a year. Although by the mid-1950s the water fountain disappeared and this source of revenue with it.

The Stockton Police Department often helped the theater; but on a regular basis, such as the Saturday matinee when there was a high volume of children and

FRANK ESAU was a member of the Mickey Mouse Club in Redding. After serving in World War II, Esau worked for Eastside Patrol. His assignment included controlling teenage rowdiness at the Fox.

teens, the theater contracted with private security. One such weekend security personnel was Frank Esau who, right after World War II in the mid-1940s, landed a job with the East Side Patrol and contracted to help at the Fox. Some of the pre-teens and teenagers on the Saturday matinees would give the private patrol problems. With hundreds of children in the theater, they would be rather mischievous and run from seat to seat. Esau picked out the noisy troublemakers and threatened to bar them from returning to the theater. Often Esau rounded up the most rowdy, took them home, and reported their behavior to their parents. Quickly many of the youngsters wised up and after the show they waited for him and he ended up providing private taxi service. As many as ten youngsters went down the street to Lyman's Restaurant on California Street to wait for Esau's generosity. Frank Esau reflected those teenagers were not malicious, just noisy.

It is difficult to list all those who have worked at the Fox at one time or another; however, many will remember the time they spent there and, invariably, they have retained fond memories of their experiences at the theater.

Sylvia Sun Minnick

Memories

I was just out of high school and my girlfriend, Wilma Brown Griffith, said, "there's a uniform that would fit you, why don't you try it." That's how I started working as an usherette. In those days all the staff worked a 48-hour week.
  — Ann Gallo Lina

I was on duty as a cashier and Vernon Ghiorzo took many nights driving back and forth along Main Street in front of the Fox in his father's 1941 Chrysler before he summoned up the courage to ask me if he could drive me home from work. Vernon had been a member of the theater's Mickey Mouse Club years before. We were married in 1943.
  — LaVerne Babcook Ghiorzo

I did not know Ann had a crush on me. She would come down to the theater just to watch me work [at the Fox] and I wasn't even dating her. Eventually we were fixed up on a blind date and I was so taken by her that night I decided to marry her.
  — Frank Esau

I said I was 16 but my true age was 15. One didn't need a work permit in those days. We were encouraged to join the Screen Actors Guild but I did not do so because the salary was only $1.00 an hour.
  — Gail Weldy Traverso

Fox had a 16MM projector and we could rent some very good shorts at reasonable rents from an outfit in Santa Rosa and we would show those along with the live talent. The longest working projectionist at the Fox was Charles Bailey who worked there from 1930 to 1969 when the Fox ended and we sold to Westland Theaters.
  — Joe Holt

The men's bathroom had overstuffed leather chairs and the women's lounge had sofas and club lounges. I also remember the high-back Spanish baroque chairs.
  — Del McComb

By 1936 Nick Turner moved on and Ray Duddy was the manager. I remember in 1965-1970 Mr. Turner, at the age of 70 or 75, came back to visit Stockton.
  — Ed Van Vranken

One time during the Ten-O-Wheel drawing, similar to roulette, Ray Duddy was drunk and, unbeknownst to him, Nick Turner, who had been promoted to San Francisco was sitting in the back of the audience and watching Duddy. Later Duddy was transferred to Bakersfield.
  — Ann Gallo Lina

Twice a year Ray Duddy picked out the money from the fish pond. Also, when he got a bit inebriated the guard fished him out because he fell in.
  — Joe Holt

I dearly loved the Fox for it reeked of history. If you go down under the stage, there's a huge box, a central vacuum that still worked; but, with the snack bar, the vacuum could not pick up the cups, popcorn boxes and so forth. The Fox bought pre-popped popcorn rather than popping them fresh.
  — Don Babcock, Manager

Chapter 6
Hollywood Comes to Stockton

The old T & D, whose name had already been changed to the Fox California three years prior, ran a double billing at its very last showing prior to demolition in 1929. The final performances at 7:00 and 9:00 p.m. featured *Manhattan Cocktail* starring Nancy Carroll and Richard Arlen. The second feature, a Zane Grey western, starred Wallace Berry, Jean Arthur and Chester Conklin in *Stairs of Sand*. A *Stockton Independent* September 10, 1929, ad announced, "Into history passes Stockton's favorite entertainment center in the years past…and in its wake rises a new and far greater link in the chain of dependable entertainment."

True to form, when the new Fox California rose one year later, management promised that the "California specializes in late releases which are shown here often before they have been seen by the public in larger cities." In conjunction with the California's policy of the latest pictures first, they would also offer on various occasions live performances. This policy entertained thousands and, more importantly, allowed Stocktonians to be a part of the growing enthusiasm for entertainment. Moviegoers followed the latest and hottest trends in music, clothing styles and jargon. They idolized captivating stars of the silver screen while learning a smattering of literature, history and geography; until then often learned only through books.

Advertisements in the local newspapers announcing the feature films appeared more alluring with sketches of leading ladies locked in romantic embrace or male stars facing imminent danger. The

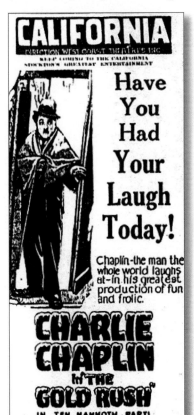

1926

1926

Jerry Sola Collection

CONCHITA MONTENEGRO was another very popular Latina star of the 1930s. Montenegro, born in San Sebastian, Spain , appeared in the 1931 *Cisco Kid*, a Fox western which had its world premiere in Stockton during the Fox's first anniversary.

mid-1920s is best remembered as the heyday of the silent stars. Among those included Charlie Chaplin, Buster Keaton, Laurel and Hardy, Douglas Fairbanks, Mary Pickford, Corrine Griffith, Norma Shearer and Greta Garbo.

By the Thirties sound greatly improved and the popularity of some silent stars quickly faded as their voices did not fit the audience's perceptions which had been formed from reading the screen to actually hearing them speak. Some stars actually preferred the silent screen such as Hungarian-born Vilma Banke, well known in America as well as in Europe. However, Banke had a very heavy Hungarian accent and did not want to do speaking roles and thus quit.

Shirley Temple became America's darling as she danced and sang lyrics containing sagacious advice in the most innocent of smiles, sparkling eyes, dimples and bobbing blond ringlets. Mothers quickly put their daughters in Mary Jane shoes,

changed their hair style and dressed them into Shirley Temple look-alikes. Teenagers and young adults took readily to the Andy Hardy series with Mickey Rooney and Judy Garland. These were immensely popular and cheap to make. Heartthrobs such as Clark Gable, James Cagney, Jimmy Stewart and Gary Cooper proved their versatility as did the female actresses who demonstrated their ability to be sultry and seductive. Gloria Swanson's role as Norma Desmond in Sunset Boulevard (1949) brought out the unabashed and unpleasant side of mental derangement, up to this time a topic not for public discussion. Older fans preferred Janet Gaynor, Marie Dressler and Wallace Beery while the younger folks were taken by Clark Gable and Jean Harlow. Mae West attracted those from ages 6 to 60.

Audiences hungered to learn more about exotic places. The *Daily Independent's* front page of May 1931, headlined *Trader Horn* as the "Miracle Movie of 1931" as it was filmed on location in deepest Africa. Not surprisingly the Tarzan movies had universal appeal for adventure

Jerry Sola Collection

LUPE VELEZ, a fiery Mexican actress co-starred with Gary Cooper in *The Wolf Song*, a 1929 Paramount romance. Velez was described as tempestuous, voluptuous and full of energy. She married Johnny "Tarzan" Weissmuller in 1933 and divorced him in 1938. She appeared in what was dubbed the Mexican "Spitfire" series.

and family viewing. Even the fictitious land well beyond the high mountains of the Himalayas evoked a sense of everlasting youth for the senior citizen as they became enthralled with Ronald Coleman and Jane Wyatt in *Lost Horizon*.

There was a continual touch of Hispanic influence aside from the mission architecture at the Fox. Hollywood in the 1930s and 40s became captivated with some of the Latina actresses such as Lupe Velez,

Conchita Montenegro and Deloris Del Rio. Aside from usherettes adopting a "Lupe Velez" uniform, Velez was known as a fiery Mexican actress and often described as tempestuous, voluptuous and full of energy. Velez is best remembered playing opposite Gary Cooper in *Wolf Song*. She married Johnny "Tarzan" Weissmuller in 1933 and divorced him in 1938. Quite observant, she had quipped in her summary of men, "the first time you buy a house you see how pretty the paint is and buy it. The second time you look to see if the basement has termites. It's the same with men."

Jerry Sola Collection

A sheet music from the movie *Caliente* starring Dolores Del Rio, Pat O'Brien and Leo Carillo in the 1935 Busby Berkeley musical.

At the first anniversary of the new Fox Theater, the feature movie *Cisco Kid* starred Conchita Montenegro with Warner Baxter and Edmund Lowe. Montenegro hailed from San Sebastian, Spain. Deloris Del Rio was an even more popular actress and she came from Durango, Mexico. She was described as one of the most beautiful women to ever appear in American movies. Viewers will remember Del Rio in *Flying Down to Rio*, a film intended as a vehicle especially written for her but, unfortunately, the limelight focused on the first appearance of the Fred Astaire and Ginger Rogers dance team. Del Rio eventually felt stereotyped and returned to Mexico where she continued her film career and received critical success. She died in 1983. Ramon Navarro also became a Latin heartthrob when he played opposite Jeannette MacDonald in *The Cat and the Fiddle* which showed at the Fox in 1934. Navarro, born Ramon Gil Samaniego in Mexico, migrated to Los Angeles and worked as an extra in various films. He became so successful, especially with women, that Hollywood began billing him as the new Valentino.

Jerry Sola Collection

RAMON NOVARRO is shown here with Jeanette MacDonald in *The Cat and the Fiddle*, a 1934 film.

Movie houses made a concerted effort to diversify their genre and gave their followers a good mix of dramas, musicals and comedy. One such example was the showing of the Oscar-winning drama "*The Good Earth*" starring Luise Rainer and Paul Muni which was then followed by another MGM production "*Broadway Melody of 1938*," with Robert Taylor, Eleanor Powell, Sophie Tucker Judy Garland and a cast of hundreds.

The theater was generally packed on holidays particularly on New Year's Eve, Christmas and Thanksgiving and management arranged for films that would be popular. One film that played on Christmas Day in 1938 was *Say It In French*, a Paramount comedy starring Ray Milland and Olympe Bradna. In 1941 she married Douglas Wilhoit, Senior and is the mother of former San Joaquin County Supervisor Douglas Wilhoit, Jr.

While foreign lands and foreign influences brought excitement, movies

Jerry Sola Collection

A lobby card such as this one was used for display in the theater's interior. *Say It In French*, a 1938 Paramount comedy, starring Ray Milland and Olympe Bradna, played in Stockton on Christmas Day, 1938. Olympe Bradna became the future wife of Douglas Wilhoit, Senior.

Jerry Sola Collection

Mandalay played at the Fox California on March 29, 1934. The newspaper ad read, "Photographed and Produced in Stockton, [the story of] One woman Alone in a Land of Desperate Men. Here's Romance That Burns, Drama That Thunders…Filled with the Magic and Madness of the Tropics." Stockton had never been classified as having a tropical ambience.

filmed on location on the San Joaquin delta and within the county, as well as Stockton itself, drew crowds anxious to identify with the scenery. Others wanted to see themselves or friends who were hired as extras. Still others went for the pure enjoyment of a good story. One of the first movies filmed in Stockton was *Mandalay* which played at the Fox on May 29, 1934. The newspaper ad read, "Photographed and produced in Stockton…the story of one woman alone in a land of desperate men. Here's Romance that burns, drama that thunders…filled with the Magic and Madness of the Tropics." The movie starred Kay Francis, Ricardo Cortez, Warner Oland and Lyle Talbut. More than likely the scenes were of the rustic area around the delta rather than in the heart of the city. Far fetched, perhaps, but the Fox had banners posted downtown to draw the crowd.

The following year in 1935 more than 350 locals appeared as extras in *Steamboat 'Round the Bend,* also filmed in Stockton. The Stockton premiere in August had a double benefit for the moviegoers: a locally shot film and the pleasure of an air conditioned movie house. The theater was packed mostly to see the climatic scene of a steamboat race that was filmed at Buckley's Cove. The excitement of the film was bittersweet in that Will Rogers, the bigger-than-life star, and his pilot Wiley Post, were killed in a plane crash near Point Barrow, Alaska just one week before the premiere.

Jerry Sola Collection

WILL ROGERS at the helm starred in *Steamboat 'Round the Bend.*

Jerry Sola Collection

Some of the cast and crew of *Steamboat 'Round the Bend,* a 1935 Fox drama, was filmed in Stockton. It had its world premiere at the Fox California on August 22, 1935. Just one week prior, Will Rogers and his pilot were killed in a plane crash near Point Barrow, Alaska.

Filming of *All The King's Men* in 1948 brought fame to Stockton. There were scenes of the County Courthouse, City Hall, Stockton Hotel, Hunter Square, the Stockton Channel, Atherton's Cove and a spectacular accident scene near Five Mile House on Lower Sacramento Road. This film, adapted from Robert Penn Warren's Pulitzer Prize winning novel about a Huey Long-character, won three academy awards for Best Picture, Best Actor Broderick Crawford, and Best Supporting Actress Mercedes McCambridge. Three local citizens,

Jerry Sola Collection

A scene from *All the King's Men*, a 1949 movie filmed in front of the Hotel Stockton. Many Stocktonians served as extras and a few had speaking parts.

Public Defender Anthony Chargin, attorney Louis Arbios and police officer Wendell Shriver had minor roles with the latter actually having a speaking part. While the premiere showing occurred at the Esquire Theater on New Year's Eve in 1949, the film did eventually play at the Fox California some forty-three years later, in 1993, as a benefit for Stockton Beautiful, a local non-profit beautification organization.

Color became a popular medium in the Forties. *Gone With The Wind* was one of the early forerunners and a major color epic. With the caliber of Clark Gable, Vivian Leigh, Olivia de Havilland, Leslie Howard and the strong story line of Margaret Mitchell's Civil War as a backdrop, this 1939 four-hour long MGM Selznick captured four Oscars for Best Picture, Best Actress Vivian Leigh, Best Supporting Actress Hattie McDaniel and Best Director Victor Fleming. It made its debut at the Fox on February 29, 1940. Cold and foggy, the doors opened at 7:30 a.m. and an hour later the house was filled even though the showing did not begin until 9:45. To this day many remember that the lines were so long they wrapped around the block down San Joaquin Street. The second showing found that some people even brought their lunch as they waited in line.

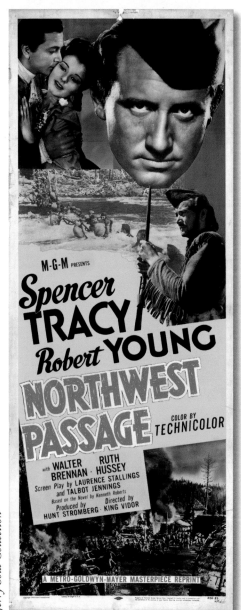

Jerry Sola Collection

A 1940 MGM film based on the real-life exploits of Rogers' Rangers, a force of 600 colonial frontiersmen starring Spencer Tracy, Robert Young and Walter Brennan.

Also in the Fall of 1940 the Fox celebrated its tenth anniversary with *Strike Up The Band*, a MGM Busby Berkeley musical starring Mickey Rooney, Judy Garland and Paul Whiteman and his orchestra. Manager Ray Duddy handed the one millionth and one ticket to Mrs. Marie Evans who had also purchased one of the first tickets when the Fox opened in 1930. Mayor Woodrow Coale cut a birthday cake as part of the festivities.

Sale of war bonds and war-related displays at the Fox drew the audience as did the war theme movies such as *Flying Tigers, Little Tokyo USA, Casablanca,* the Warner Bros. hit starring Humphrey

Bogart and Ingrid Bergman, and *This is the Army,* the 1943 musical by Irving Berlin that included a young lieutenant Ronald Reagan. While Hollywood was cranking out patriotic-theme movies, the road shows of Bing Crosby, Bob Hope and Dorothy Lamour beginning with *The Road to Morocco* lightened up the country's spirit. During the filming of *The Road to Utopia,* the cast, including the three mega-stars, made a brief stop at the Stockton Airport in 1945.

All during the years of World War II, the big bands made many appearances in Stockton. A feature movie accompanied the live orchestra performance, thus giving the audience their money's worth. Ted Lewis, Dorsey, Miller, Harry James, Paul Whiteman and others came to town. Duke Ellington appeared on stage on May 28, 1942, for a matinee as well as an evening performance. While the Fox had live performances, a few of the great headliners also entertained at the University of the Pacific Auditorium or the Stockton High Auditorium. If the big band music was conducive to dancing, the event then was held at the Civic Auditorium. More frequently the Fox booked Fanchon and Marco Revues. The creators were a brother-sister ballroom dance team turned promoter-producers of stage shows. They had five separate groups of dancers who rotated in different

theaters from Los Angeles to Vancouver.

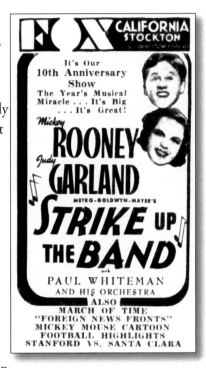

Fox West Coast Theaters by the mid-Forties owned not only the Fox California but also two others, the Ritz and the State. Often when a movie had the first run at the Fox California the same film could then be seen at the other two theaters on subsequent runs. Film companies almost exclusively showed their movies in theaters they owned or controlled. The Ritz ran MGM movies, the Fox played those of Warner Brothers, 20th Century Fox and Paramount while the Esquire showed Universal, Columbia Pictures and United Artist films.

On August 18, 1943, Irving Berlin's *This is the Army* was shown to benefit the Army Emergency Relief. The movie featured many Warner Bros. stars including George Murphy, Joan Leslie and young Lt. Ronald Reagan. Kate Smith sang *God Bless America,* and her rendition remained the most stirring version ever performed.

Jerry Sola Collection

Sheet music from the 1942 classic *Casablanca* with Humphrey Bogart, Ingrid Bergman, and others. Dooley Wilson's memorable version of this song is one of the highlights of the film.

Bank of Stockton Archives

While filming the *Road to Utopia*, some of the cast and crew stopped at the Stockton Airport. Identifiable are Bing Crosby, Bob Hope and Gary Cooper standing to the right of Dorothy Lamour (hidden by the hat). Circa 1946.

Because of these divisions many of the films made on location locally from 1950s onward were premiered elsewhere than the Fox.

The Stockton Theater on Pacific Avenue just north of Harding Way opened its doors in 1950. Intended to be a neighborhood theater, it, nevertheless, redirected the moviegoers northward and most of the movie houses downtown felt the loss, particularly the Fox California. Eventually the Stockton Theater, later renamed the Stockton Royal, also lost its attendance number when still more movie houses moved farther north into shopping malls and shopping complexes.

Jerry Sola Collection

Lobby card, *Show Boat*, 1951 MGM musical, starring Kathryn Grayson, Ava Gardner, Howard Keel and others. Notable songs included *My Bill*, *Can't Help Lovin' Dat Man*, *Old Man River*, and *Make Believe*.

Jerry Sola Collection

Sheet music from the 1952 movie, *With A Song In My Heart*, about Jane Froman, a USO volunteer who survived a plane crash in 1943 and entertained the troops throughout Europe.

Anchors Aweigh, a 1945 MGM musical about sailors on leave, starring Frank Sinatra, Gene Kelly, Kathryn Grayson and Jose Iturbi. This was an era when musicals became extremely popular.

Hollywood and major production companies continued to come to Stockton and San Joaquin County to shoot on location. One was *Big Country* (1958) filmed on a ranch east of Farmington where there were no visible fences or power lines. This starred Gregory Peck, Charlton Heston, Jean Simmons, Charles Bickford and Burl Ives.

Porgy and Bess did play at the Fox. This movie, filmed in 1959 and using the San Joaquin delta, starred Sidney Portier, Dorothy Dandridge, Pearl Bailey, Sammy Davis, Jr. and Diahann Carroll among others. This production had an important impact on the local economy as evidenced by a headline in the *Stockton Record* of September 10, 1958, which read "Advance crew…spent $10,950 in eight days." Having screen stars frequent local restaurants and pumping money into the local economy gave the city a big boost.

Porgy and Bess provided an insight into the long hours it took shooting on location, often as much as twelve straight hours. Almost two weeks later the newspaper on September 27th reported on the progress of the film stating that the delta island was easily transformed into "Catfish Row." As it further stated, "[A] riotous

picnic in the tradition of the Old South was filmed here because, according to Otto Preminger, the film director, the original setting for *Porgy and Bess* was in Charleston, South Carolina in 1912 and it no longer looked as it did then." Purportedly, Sammy Davis, Jr. wanted the role of Sportin' Life so badly he offered to do it for nothing. However, Samuel Goldwyn, who had heard Davis sing two of the show's songs in a Hollywood nightclub,

Jerry Sola Collection

Judy Garland had two major musicals premiere in 1948, *Easter Parade* with Fred Astaire and *The Pirate* with Gene Kelley. Garland had moved on from her days with Mickey Rooney and the *Andy Hardy* series.

Bank of Stockton Archives

The Big Country cast members; Chuck Connors, Jean Simmons and Charlton Heston pose with restaurant owner Peter L. Massei at the Reef Tavern on Pacific Avenue in 1958.

Bank of Stockton Archives

While filming *Porgy and Bess*, Sammy Davis, Jr. had an opportunity to visit with UOP football star Dick Bass in 1958.

went backstage and offered Davis the role without a screen test. Several unforgettable melodies became musical classicals "*Summertime*", "*It Ain't Necessarily So*," and "*I got Plenty of Nothin'*."

Don Babcock, the former manager of the Stockton Theater and also the manager of the Fox California in the 1970s, remembered clearly *Big Country*, *God's Little Acre* and *High Times*. After a day's shoot the film was flown down to Los Angeles and the following day the cast, crew, and big-name stars anxiously went to the Stockton Theater to see the rushes.

Without a doubt the Fox California held the greatest memories for moviegoers because of the beauty of the theater, that definitive time in their lives, and the experience of seeing such great classics as *Moby Dick*, Grapes *of Wrath*, *Showboat*, *Damn Yankees*, and the 1960 thriller *Psycho* starring Janet Leigh, the hometown favorite. The Fox had a fabulous forty years but times were changing and so was the downtown.

Sylvia Sun Minnick

Bank of Stockton Archives

Jo Van Fleet played *Cool Hand Luke's* mother and studied drama at UOP under Professor Demarcus Brown. She won an Oscar in 1955.

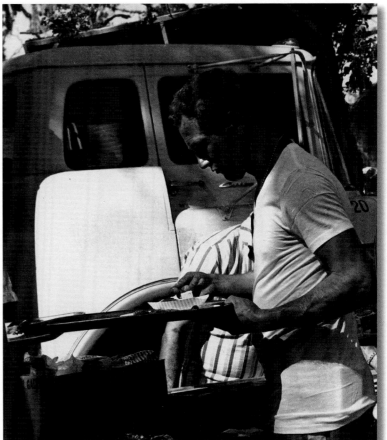

Bank of Stockton Archives

Paul Newman in *Cool Hand Luke*, a 1967 drama filmed near Stockton. Notably funny was the egg-eating contest.

Fox Remembered

When producers came to Stockton in 1973 looking for extras for the TV movie *Remember When*, I enthusiastically signed up. The movie was about a family's ordeal at home while favorite sons fought World War II abroad. It starred Jack Warden, Tim Matheson and Robbie Benson, but I can't remember when or where it aired.

I do remember showing up for work on a cold November morning and being instructed by the First Assistant Director to get a haircut. After being traumatically shorn of my long hair— this was the 70's, remember—I was sent to wardrobe where I was put in a tweed overcoat, orange scarf and baggy flannel slacks.

After six hours of shooting at a church on Center Street, we moved downtown to the Fox Theater. This was during Fox's relatively dormant period, as multiplexes on the north side siphoned moviegoers and the grand old venue was relegated to closed circuit telecasts of heavyweight fights and concerts of long forgotten Bay Area rock bands.

It still had the gilded pillars and the flowing staircase in the lobby, but I remember it looking tired. As a boy, I saw *It's a Mad, Mad, Mad, Mad World* there and *Mary Poppins*, too. The movie-going experience at the Fox was as epic as the production on screen. There was a heavy velvet curtain eclipsing the screen and crystal chandeliers and faux opera boxes and red carpet and a balcony with a seating capacity bountiful enough to host it's own Broadway play. There are still some great movie theaters where I live now in Los Angeles; the Westwood and Egyptian and Mann's Chinese jump to mind, but I'd put the Fox in its glory days (and now renaissance) up there with any of them.

The first scene we shot at the Fox was in the balcony. I sat in the dark and was instructed to smoke a cigarette through ten takes. We then went downstairs to shoot the lobby and the director deputized me to be actor Tim Matheson's stand-in. This required me to go where the actor would go as the cinematographer set up lighting and rehearsed camera moves.

I had been working nine tediously boring hours and welcomed the change. For me, the magic of Hollywood had long since worn off. I had calculated that I would never be seen on camera, because I was always off in the distance when the director called "Action." And the only time I was close to the lens, I was in the dark watching a movie. And that hideous haircut. Whitewall above the ears! I dreaded going to school the next day.

But then my luck changed. There was this girl I had been eyeing since we had moved to the Fox location. She was dressed as a candy vendor, circa 1944. Tight red curls, little cap tilted to the side, fitted dress. I had wanted to talk to her for some time, but she only started noticing me when I got bumped up to stand-in and the crew fussed over where I should walk and stand. Finally, I mustered up the courage and approached the girl behind the candy counter in the lobby. Picture me in tweed coat and scarf, her in vintage movie-vendor uniform, heavy make-up reflecting the style of the period. I learn her name's Julie and she's studying drama at Delta—"Hey, so am I"—and we seem to be hitting it off. She laughed at my jokes, or maybe it was my hair, all I know is I had some game going that night.

And then I noticed her eyes fall off me, followed by a sudden slackening of all her facial muscles. Someone had walked up behind me. It was the movie's star, Tim Matheson. Tim was drop-dead handsome, with a winning smile and to this day women still swoon over him.

Tim just leaned on the counter, flashed those baby blues at Julie and asked her about her life. I suddenly disappeared off Julie's radar and no one was sending out a search plane.

I went outside to smoke a cigarette and kick-off a five-year habit. I ended up making $13.50 for fifteen hours of work and I didn't get the girl.

Cut to 28 years later and I'm a producer on *The West Wing* standing outside Stage 26 at Warner Brothers talking to the man who played the Vice President on the show, Tim Matheson. I tell him about *Remember When* and Stockton and how he stole Julie from me in the lobby of the Fox. He shakes his head, says he doesn't remember taking my girl.

"All I remember about that day was that we shot inside this beautiful theater."

Many things are forgettable in life, like say TV movies and extras in ill-fitting tweed. The Fox Theater isn't one of them.

— Kevin Falls,
  September 8, 2004

Memories

My father was a cowboy actor in Hollywood and was in many Hopalong Cassidy pictures.
    — Frank Esau

I began going to the Fox California by myself at the age of 7 or 8. In 1948 or 49, I saw Blue Lagoon *with British actress Jean Simmons. When I was 9 in the 1950s, there was* Annie Get Your Gun, *1951* Showboat *with Ava Gardner, Howard Keel and Kathryn Grayson;* Ivanhoe *with Robert Taylor, Elizabeth Taylor and Joan Fontaine and the reissue of* Gone With the Wind. *I was pushed "over the edge" in 1955 when I saw a re-release of* The Wizard of Oz. *That's when I became a real movie lover and started my collection of movie memorabilia. The fascination continues to this day.*
    — Jerry Sola

When I saw the Earl White Scandal, *stage show, I thought the women were disrobing and immediately the thought crossed my mind as "oh my," but, it was not really disrobing.*
    — Don Babcock

My buddy, Dave Ratto and I went to see Planet of the Apes *and* Planet of the Vampires. *We were so scared that we left in the middle of the movies.*
    — Mike Fitzgerald

Chapter 7
Weathering a Storm

Stockton's downtown was on a rapid decline. Many social changes occurred in the 1950s starting with a tremendous migration northward. The city's incremental annexation process acquired new lands north of the Calaveras River creating residential areas in Lincoln Village and Weberstown. Affordable automobiles allowed families to move into bigger houses with larger backyards and shop in the suburban malls rather than downtown. Even the local community college made plans to build a much larger complex north of the river on the old state hospital farmland. People no longer depended on public transportation to shop downtown. Some of the original storeowners barely hung on, others abandoned generations of family enterprise and sought work elsewhere. Downtown had its own woe - the lack of parking spaces. It was easier to drive to the new theaters and park in big parking lots that were free. Even if one did not want to leave his car, motor movies on the outskirts of town came into being. Thus, going downtown and to the Fox Theater was no longer a "big deal." Television became the bane as the family huddled within the comfort of their living room and became glued to such programs as *The Ed Sullivan Show*, *Milton Berle*, or *The Colgate Hour*.

Courtesy of Don Babcock

RODDA HARVEY was president of Westland Theaters. He built the Stockton Theater on Pacific Avenue in 1945 and by 1970 bought the lease to the Fox and held it for ten years.

DON BABCOCK went to work at the Stockton Theater starting as a door man in 1950 and through the years moved up the corporate ladder to become the vice president and general manager of Harvey Amusement Corporation. His duties included managing the Fox among the other theaters owned by the corporation.

The movie business also underwent major changes and quite rapidly at that. In 1951 Fox, Warner Bros., and Lowes (MGM) were sued in restraint of trade and the movie companies were ordered to divest themselves of their theaters. The 20th Century-owned or controlled movie houses became National General Theaters. Local management also changed as Ray Duddy left in the early 1960s for Bakersfield and Don

Crook became the new manager. National General's problem was difficult to solve; it could not get first run movies and it would not lower the admission fee. As hard as Crook tried, revenues declined. He slowly reduced the large and faithful Fox staff and the building began to fall into disrepair. Gail Weldy remembers when she worked the candy counter in 1958. The staff dressing room stored the popcorn and she had to change into her uniform quickly as the mice were in there at the same time.

The Fox's major competition in the early 1950s was the Stockton Theater on Pacific Avenue owned by Rodda Harvey, president of the Westland Theaters. Harvey arrived in Stockton in 1944, and was also operating film houses in the Bay Area, Visalia and other parts of Northern California. By the mid-1960s Harvey bought the Esquire Theater on Main Street where he brought first run movies including the local premiering of *Cool Hand Luke*, the movie filmed in Stockton and starred Paul Newman. Harvey kept the Esquire for a few years; however, the city's redevelopment effort acquired the land for municipal parking and also an enlargement of the Union Safe Deposit Bank on Main Street.

By 1971 Harvey acquired both the Fox and the Ritz for $25,000, and he honored the Wilhoit family's land lease. Harvey's general manager Don Babcock shuffled films between the different theaters as long as there was an audience.

While the best attendance days occurred on holidays, such as Thanksgiving, Christmas and New Years, the majority of those who came were youngsters from low income families. Trouble frequently occurred when the youngsters preferred to loiter in the lobby rather than vacate the premises after the feature movie. On one Christmas Day, Babcock remembers distinctly the movie was James Bond's 007 *Goldfinger*, and some of the young men started a commotion. Babcock, somehow or other, got burned in the back of his ear with a cigarette. Collaring the young man and asking him to leave, the response from the youngster was, "Mister, if you had a home like mine, you won't go home either."

In November of 1969 real violence shook the Fox and its neighboring shops. Some 230 youths rioted in the theater and they poured into the streets, teasing police dogs and breaking store windows. Four months later, on March 15, 1970 when a private patrolman attempted to eject a youth who was walking down the aisle with a radio playing full blast, a free-for-all

developed. The police sent 1,300 screaming patrons into the street where they again broke store windows and blocked traffic for an hour. Seven youths, ages 12 to 17 years of age and three adults were arrested.

When the theater security was not able to control the crowd and the attendance got in the thousands, Babcock called upon individuals in the Black community for help. One such person was Edison High School football coach Ben Parks who later went on to be Joe Montana's personal trainer and, ultimately, the trainer for the 49er Team. Another who was called upon to keep the rowdy youngsters in line was Edna Macon, the daughter of Eddie Macon. Her father, Eddie, had been a wide receiver at the University of the Pacific and went on to play for the Chicago Bears. Edna was an usherette at the Esquire. She, like her father, was very tall and slim. Her height was fairly impressive and Edna had a special way of dealing with the teenagers. She was so good that even the other theaters, including the Fox and the Ritz, asked for her frequently for crowd control. She would then march down the street in her Esquire uniform and handle the situation. After about an hour she would return to her station.

Business was not good and by 1973 Rodda Harvey lamented, "…the business was 'terrible' in the downtown theater." He hoped the house would be rented for live entertainment." Even Helen Flynn, reporter for the *Stockton Record* on February 25, 1973, decried,

[The] center of town is often deserted at night. Much of the accoutrements for opening night [at the Fox] are now shabby and sooty. Several sections closed off to the public. Upstairs lounge where overflow crowds waited still has the fireplace but no furniture of any kind and no one, not even the owners, seem to know where it went. Toilets in the upstairs lounge have been pulled out and the floors cemented. Nobody seems to know who did that either. The grand organ can't be found and the lobby or foyer no longer has the beautiful fountain, most of the beautiful touches of the palace remain under a shabby covering at the moment. All the equipment in the projection room at the top of the theater is still in excellent condition. Movies are shown daily and the acoustics are excellent. Harvey estimates it would cost $150,000 to refurbish the Fox.

The Fox was in a deplorable state. Tickets were $2.00 for adults, $1.50 for juniors and 50 cents for children, and even with these lower prices the theater could not get much of an audience. Since the major film companies no longer controlled the theaters, their film rental policies took a bigger share of the profits. Twenty years previous, a movie house could rent two films, a first run and a second feature, for about $5,000. By the early 1970s for first run film the theater had to guarantee and upfront the rental cost which could be between $20,000 to as much as $200,000. The scale also fluctuated based on the lease time. The standard was to give the production company seventy percent of the take, twenty percent for operating costs and the house kept ten percent. The older the film, the less the rental cost. Unquestionably, the movie house relied on the candy concession to make up the profit.

As bad as it was, Harvey tried a variety of live entertainment, including signing on Family Production which gave two rock and roll concerts in 1973 and

PERFECTO MARQUEZ, one of Jesse's sons, who took over the managerial and projectionist duties at the Fox in the mid-1970s.

Courtesy of David Marquez

1974. These were single night events. While there were individuals who praised the efforts and the tickets sold for $4.00 and $2.00 for students, it still was not enough. In the mid-1970s the Fox tried televised fights which were booked through sport companies and coaxial cables were brought into the theater. The "Thriller in Manila", the third in a series of fights between Mohammed Ali and Joe Frasier gave the theater a big boost. Filipinos, Blacks Mexicans and others in the boxing community packed the audience. The snack bar was a big hit, beer was the attraction. Since the theater did not have a liquor license an outside concessionaire ran that part of the business. The fight was so well advertised a soon-to-be city council member was outside of the theater taking bets. The consensus was that although Ali won, the fight was not really that good.

On September 22, 1975, fight aficionados paid $8.00 each to see three closed-circuit fights. But, the third match was cancelled because of disturbances not in the Fox, but at the LA Coliseum, the fight site. Those in the Fox Theatre were incensed because they were not getting their money's worth and two hundred of the patrons milled around the theater and broke two

windows. No arrest was made, however, three men were briefly detained.

Harvey also experimented with Latino movies and received moderate return during the summer months when students were out of school and the farm workers took up residence in town. Harvey was willing to try other forms of live entertainment. At the same time he put out feelers that he might close the Fox in hopes that his other theaters, including the Ritz, could balance out his corporation's revenue.

One of Harvey's employees, Jose "Jesse" Marquez grasped the American dream. Marquez, who emigrated

JOSE "JESSE" MARQUEZ emigrated from Mexico and worked as a custodian for Rodda Harvey. He learned enough of the theater maintenance business to sublease the Fox for Mexican films. The Marquez operation at the Fox was a family affair.

Courtesy of David Marquez

from Mexico, worked for Harvey as a custodian for many years. The families became close and the Marquez children enjoyed dipping in Harvey's pool and staying at his cabin in the foothills. Marquez offered to sublet Harvey's lease and take over the management of the Fox and run Hispanic movies which, to him, seemed to be a lucrative

NINA MARQUEZ and GLORIA ROSA worked the concession stand.

Courtesy of David Marquez

business. Marquez gave the Fox a new name " Sus Elegante Theatro Fox" – Your Elegant Fox Theater. As the *Stockton Record* indicated, "Peace came to the Fox in 1976 with the Spanish-language films and a new name."

Marquez and his two sons, Perfecto and David, took out a fictitious name notice in the *Stockton Record* in late 1975. Little did they anticipate the difficulty,

On December 12, 1976 this photo was taken in front of the concession stand with the workers Maria and Rosa Gloria and Elsa and Sylvia Marquez.

and, yet, the joy of private enterprise. This became a true family affair. Marquez' wife Ramona and the other children Eva, Sylvia and Maria Elena, including cousins Elsa and Linda quickly rolled up their sleeves and took part in a variety of duties. Oldest son, Perfecto, took over the managerial and projectionist duties while the women managed the food concession and Jesse did all the work necessary from top to bottom. The youngest son, 17-year old David, served as the all-around helper and learned to do the paperwork.

The Marquez Family's opening night on October 12, 1975, had 751 people pay to see *Uno Y Medio Contin el Mundo Rio Salvaje*. The total day's take was $1,619.04 of which the candy counter sales amounted to $561.54. The family was elated. In the ensuing months Jesse Marquez provided Mexican films although they competed with the Capri Theater farther east on Main Street which also showed first-run Mexican movies. David Marquez thought competition was unfair. The Los Angeles distributors insisted that they submit sealed bids for the acquisition of the movies, particularly the "hot movies." Marquez did not know if they were in the running for the good shows or not. In addition they had to book these films as far in advance as

DAVID MARQUEZ, the junior all-around man and handler of all the paperwork.

three months, not knowing if the movies would be of interest to their viewers by then or forgotten in lieu of current attractions. In addition, there was suspicion of insider information regarding the bidding process for the Capri always outbid them. For a very short period the Marquez family also tried a few riskique movies but learned quickly it was not to their liking. Thus, the Marquez Family made a concerted effort to provide family-type movies and even, on occasion, booked Mexican actors and performers to appear at the Fox including Julio Aleman, Maria Velazco "La India Maria", Lorenzo de Monteclaro King Clave, and others.

A sign in the box office announced the closure of the Fox under the Marquez Family tenure. It says that the Ritz Theater, also under the stewardship of the Marquez family, would be open on Saturday, Sunday and Monday.

The Marquez family strained under the burden of running the Fox. The bills continued to mount including a sublease monthly payment of $2,000 to Harvey and an average utility bill of $1,500 to heat and cool the building. While the building was fairly cool in the summertime because of the concrete walls, heating became a far more difficult problem coaxing an antiquated boiler system. Just twenty years prior it took a staff of thirty-two full-time employees to run the theater, Marquez turned to friends and relatives for assistance. They called on Joe Holt, the former projectionist, for technical help and were grateful for the support Harvey and his other staff gave.

David said his family had true passion as well as frustration when they leased the Fox. There were idiosyncrasies of upkeep. To change the light bulbs on the lobby's majestic chandelier, he had to go up to the roof and open a hatch to reach the crank that lowered the light fixture. He remembers his father's insistence that the three alleyways leading to the Fox be washed down frequently as the homeless used these narrow passages as personal latrines. An equally unpleasant job was to clear off the pigeon droppings, feathers and even decomposed birds from the roof drain to prevent clogging and leakage into the building. Even on his wedding day, going between the church and the reception, David insisted that the wedding party make a stop at the Fox to check out the conditions at the theater including the day's attendance. It was, after all, the family business and he felt responsible.

After several years Jesse Marquez realized the Fox was too big and too expensive to handle. Rodda Harvey suggested that Jesse and his family lease the Ritz, just a block down the street and run that. The Ritz was much smaller and more in keeping with their finances. The lease was about $1,200 and the overhead much less. The facilities were more modern and there was no boiler system. The Marquez family operated the Ritz until the Spring of 1987 when the president of American Savings made them an offer for their lease and equipment and to vacate the Ritz premises. David Marquez says, "We did not take the first offer but then settled for the second." The family did not want to leave the business but they really had no choice. With some coaxing from the city which was bending over backwards to help American Savings amass the block's properties to build their corporate headquarters and property owner Andrew Wolfe's willingness to sell, it was obvious that the family was squeezed out of their livelihood.

Meanwhile by 1978 Harvey signed a one-year lease with a young promotion group from Los Angeles, Horizon Entertainment Enterprises. The new company renamed the theater Fox Theater of the Performing Arts and claimed they spent $35,000 on upgrades. Ironically,

with all the renovations and refurbishing that was done at the Fox with thousands upon thousands of dollars by past and future owners and operators, Horizon was the only one to receive an Award of Excellence from the city's Cultural Heritage Board.

They booked a series of rock concerts and claimed, "in the near future the theater is planning to offer the best of the many roads of music: jazz, country-western, pop, easy listening and rock." The company fell short of its promise. Shortly after occupying the building, Horizon was lax with the monthly rent; the deadline was extended several times. Their payments kept falling behind, in short, they operated the theater for four months but paid only two months' worth of rent. Attempts to reach the Horizon people went in vain and Harvey was forced to file an eviction notice not once but twice. Eventually, Horizon asked out of their lease, leaving Harvey in search of another tenant. An oddity occurred during Horizon's occupancy in that

Friday Feb 17, 1978

Fox Theater Operators Want Out

BY Vince Perrin
Of The Record Staff

Operators of the downtown Fox Theater of the Performing Arts who have left town with their rent unpaid, have told the theater landlord they "want out" of their one-year lease.

That is what the promoters told an attorney

then only December's rent has been paid, Babcock said.

Westland president Rodda Harvey is currently "looking into the situation," Babcock said, and a course of possible legal action may be determined by the middle of next week.

He said that spokesmen for Horizon claim that a Record story last week about the eviction notices "scared

$35,000 to renovate the historical old theater at 242 E. Main St., to make it a home for "all the performing arts." Since then it has presented two rrk concerts there, both of which drew poorly.

An initial eviction notice was sent to the theater after a monthly payment due last Dec. 1 had not been paid.

Eventually it was paid, Babcock said.

Before the Jan. 1 payment was due a Horizon spokes-

Sat. Jan 28, 1978

Fox Theater Operators Sent Second Eviction Notice—Rent Unpaid

Operators of the downtown Fox Theater of the Performing Arts this week were sent their second eviction notice in two months, according to the building's landlord, Westland

E. Main St. after a monthly payment due last Dec. 1 had not been paid. Eventually it was paid.

Before the Jan. 1 payment was due a spokesman for Horizon sought

Last October Horizon announced plans to spend $35,000 in cosmetic renovation of the historical old theater to make it a home for "all the performing arts." Since then it has

there was a break-in and burglars took the high fidelity sound speakers and other audio equipment. This left the theater totally without sound. Don Babcock said, "oddly enough…that's all that was taken. We have a theater but no sound." This new development added greatly to Harvey's overhead.

Harvey wanted the theater alive again. He even approached the City Council and the Board of Trustees of San Joaquin Delta College to turn the Fox into a true cultural center. The latter group's own facility, the Warren Atherton Auditorium, was already in the works.

BUREAUCRACY AND POLITICS

In late 1978 a group of citizens heard of a downtown redevelopment plan that called for the demolition of the Fox. To stop this dastardly deed, a small group appeared before the city's Cultural Heritage Board to gain support for a historic designation. Their next stop was the Planning Commission. Among those who attended the Planning hearing was Douglas Wilhoit, Sr., who had, by 1965, acquired fifty percent ownership of the lease from his two grandaunts. Elsie and Mary Wilhoit testified of the joy the theater had given to the community through the Depression and decades beyond. He summed up his statement by saying, "Pin a medal on the 'old girl', thank her and keep her forever," Only one commissioner dissented in the final vote.

The request for landmark designation then went forth to the City Council on December 15th, and much to everyone's surprise, the City Council unanimously rejected both of the lower bodies' recommendations. The City Council's rationale was to give Barnett-Range Corporation the ability to include the theater as part of their renovation plan for the adjacent California Building. Barnett-Range had acquired the high-rise from a San Francisco firm for $350,000. Hal Barnett, president of Barnett-Range, envisioned converting it into luxury offices. Demolishing the theater auditorium would provide parking spaces for future tenants. Meanwhile the Courthouse annex was being proposed at the west end of the same block. Both actions would

change the face and the use of the entire block. As a compromise Barnett-Range's architects thought they might be able to salvage the lobby and turn it into a financial institution.

Wednesday, Feb. 21, 1979 11

Fighting to Start in Earnest Over Fate of Fox Theater

By Vince Perrin
Of the Record Staff

Proponents and opponents have passed the point of taking sides in the controversy over the fate of the Fox California Theater in downtown Stockton. Tuesday, they took action.

"Stockton has been waiting for so many years for this to happen," he said. "If Fritz goes ahead and develops that building — he's going to do it, I know he is — you're going to see a lot of positive things happen downtown."

Opponents of Barnett's plan don't see it that way at all. They see it as a real threat to one of Stockton's most beautiful buildings, and one of the few

The Stockton Arts Commission threw in their support to save the building, however the Downtown Merchants Associates thought Barnett's plan was a good step toward a revitalization of the downtown. The issue was clearly divided and supporters on both sides spoke with equal passion. Council members stood firm and were willing to allow Barnett-Range time to finish their feasibility study and postponed any decision for several months.

The Central Parking District, the downtown arm of the city, commissioned an appraisal report by Craig Hubbard and Richard B. Bradford and they released the report in February of 1979. The appraisal was to "estimate the Just Compensation and Market Value" for the site that had frontages on three streets whose addresses were 232-242 East Main Street, 25-31 South San Joaquin Street and 231-239 East Market Street. The principle structure was the Fox California at 242 East Main and the other portions of the subject appraisal were the peripherally occupied commercial shops. Included in the report were comparative trends toward urban renewal that listed the old Alhambra Theatre, a large ornate vaudeville and movie house in Sacramento that was turned into a supermarket and parking lot and the Fox-Senator, also in Sacramento, which gave way to a new high rise office building.

The appraisal gave two estimates: 1) if there was total demolition of the Fox including all the improvements, the land value was about $100,000 and 2) if there was only a partial demolition and the lobby was retained for other use, the value approximated $195,000. The final conclusion by the appraiser was that, "after consideration of location, age, size,

Courtesy of Robert Shellenberger

A wrecking ball brought down the Yosemite Theatre. The original proscenium arch had long been hidden by a movie screen façade. This theater gave way to the Esquire Theater and was razed to make way for a parking lot in 1971.

competition, operating expenses, and potential uses, it seems relatively certain that the property no longer has an economic value as a theater property."

The February 21, 1979, *Stockton Record* had in blazing headlines, "Fighting to Start in Earnest Over Fate of Fox Theater." A lengthy description of the situation was spelled out including the various leaders of the opposing camps. Reporter Vince Perrin, stated that "the members of the Downtown Stockton Associates meeting at the Yosemite Club, across the corner from the Fox Theater, acted unanimously to support a proposal by Barnett-Range Corporation to turn the theater auditorium into a parking lot...." At the same time the Cultural Heritage Board called for an organizational meeting asking interested citizens to help save the auditorium. This meeting was set for February 28, and was led by Heritage Board Chairman Ray Hillman. The group met at the Stockton Public Library and organized themselves as Friends of the Fox. They discussed avenues to stay the wrecker's ball. Hillman, it seemed to reporter Perrin, was the only enlisted man at the ramparts. However, after an informal tour of the grand old theater by the Save the Fox support group and other interested citizens, the response was overwhelming.

A later article, also by Perrin, indicated "Condemnation looms as a real threat to what Councilman Ralph Lee White called 'a big old raggedy building." The response was "That's a rather rude remark to make about a lady who, was once toasted as the finest inland theater in California, and now has fallen upon hard times." Perrin went on to say, "Clearly, this is no way to treat a lady."

City of Stockton Files

Confirmation of Fox California Theatre's application received and entered in the National Registry of Historic Places.

On May 24th one hundred and forty people who opposed Barnett's plan attended the public meeting held at the theater. As background information they learned that condemnation is legal only if it is undertaken for a "100 percent public project." Since Barnett's plan was for private purposes, the question arose about the legality of the condemnation.

The last week of May was a busy week. The Friends of the Fox filed nomination papers to put the theater on the National Register of Historical Places and by that action the building could not be razed until a public meeting occurred in Washington, D.C. Meanwhile *Hot Jam* a local bluegrass group performed at the Fox to demonstrate the theater's excellent acoustics. This was followed by still other live performances by the Paul Whiteman and Tommy Dorsey bands.

At the next council meeting on May 29th, by a vote of 6 to 3, the City Council authorized the condemnation of the Fox as well as the three adjoining downtown buildings to make room for a 75-space public parking lot. The vote came just before 2:00 A.M. following a four-hour testimony by thirty-two individuals (nineteen in opposition). Several representatives from the California Historical Resources Commission from Sacramento spoke in support of the Fox. The council members who voted for the condemnation were Jack Clayton, Tom Madden, James Paige, Daniel A. O'Brien, Ennis Ramos and Ralph Lee White. Mayor Arnold Rue, Vice Mayor Jesse Nabors and council member William Sousa voted against the motion. The Editorial on May 31, 1979, indicated the *Stockton Record* was supportive of the City Council's motion and thought "[the] Council took appropriate action. Barnett's proposal comes as the third significant redevelopment step in the downtown in recent months, joining the Schmitz waterfront plan and the purchase of the Bank of America building on Main Street by the Grupe Company." It continues, "...progress always produces some victims as it produces rewards."

Attorney Barbara Fass, representing the owner of the 62-year old Central Building at 15-21 South San Joaquin Street (next to the California Building) challenged the legality of the condemnation action through a court suit. Richard Konig, attorney for the co-owner of the Fox considered joining the legal challenge. The case went before Superior Court Judge William Biddick, Jr. in July who halted the demolition plans. The judge ruled that an Environmental Impact

Report should have been considered by the City before the Council took their action of May 29th.

By July 5, 1979, the State Office of Historical Preservation, the California arm of the National Register, received the document that the Fox California Theater was now on the National Register of Historical Places. The state agency now also provided the theater a state historical landmark status.

Simultaneously, there was a whirlwind of title changes associated with the land. By May 31st Westland Theaters' lease had expired and the land use reverted back to the owners. The succession of land ownership by the middle of 1979 changed to Edward Merlo and Madelyn Lawton. They asked the court to order the City Council to rescind their "Resolution of Necessity." The owners claimed they had a vested interest in their property and such proceedings violated their constitutional rights to protection of their property without due process. With that action the City Council's new motion rescinded their previous action.

The fight for the Fox was over. She was no longer in danger of demolition and instead of being vulnerable, she became venerable. The Fox California had reached a milestone - fifty years – and now was recognized by Stockton, California, and the United States as a historic landmark. However much she was loved for her architecture, or perhaps because she symbolized

10-4-79

Fox Theater Gets Historic Status

The Fox California Theater, which has been fighting off the wrecker's ball, has been placed on the National Register of Historical Places and is being recommended by the state Historical Resources Commission for registration as a state historical landmark.

The Fox opened in 1930 as the largest vaudeville house in California, although the Paramount Theater in Oakland, completed in 1932, subsequently took that distinction away from the Stockton structure.

In 1977, the theater was leased by Horizon Entertainment Enterprises

of Los Angeles and was renamed Fox Theater of the Performing Arts. But, according to Westland Theaters manager Don Babcock, the promoters left town with their rent unpaid in early 1978 and asked that they be freed from their one-year lease.

The Fox's encounter with the wrecker's ball began looming this past February when Barnett-Range Corp. proposed to turn the theater auditorium into a parking lot for a planned adjacent luxury office building. The Downtown Stockton Associates unanimously supported the developers' plans to demolish the

theater to aid in the plan to renovate the California Building into a luxury facility at a cost of $1.5 million.

The City Council took action May 29 that could begin condemnation proceedings, and city officials are awaiting an environmental impact report on the developers' proposal. However, Superior Court Judge William Biddick Jr. gave the theater a reprieve in July, halting proceedings until the environmental report is considered. The judge said the city should have obtained such a report before taking its May 29 action.

elements of past events in people's lives, she continued to bear signs of arrested decay for several more decades. It would have to be the owners and others who came in contact with her to generate the passion and extraordinary effort to sustain her past those fifty years.

Sylvia Sun Minnick

Mi Elegante Fox Theatre

In the Fall of 1975 I was 17 years old and just out of high school. I was at the fork of my life with three choices – join the military service, enter college or become an adventurous businessperson. I chose the latter and on October 12, 1975, my life was never the same.

My parents worked for Westland Theaters, Inc. for many years as custodians and in the maintenance department. My older brother, three sisters and I helped our parents. As Westland Theaters tapped into the Spanish movie market, the owners offered us an opportunity to assist them in operating this venture. Since we were familiar with the movie theater business, we agreed to lease the Fox Theatre and run it as a family venture.

We opened for business on October 12, 1975 with a grand welcome and success thanks to our patrons. I remember that night before going to bed all the excitement and thrill of show business that I experienced that day and knew I was set for a whole new perspective in life. I found that most of the skills in running a movie theater were not something you learn in school, but, more on a day-by-day basis. I, then, decided it was time to enter college and major in Business Administration so I could help the business along and for back up in the event I had to pursue other options in the future.

The Jesse Marquez family operated the Fox Theatre from October 1975 through 1979. We offered different Mexican Spanish movies three days a week. From time to time there were also live performances with famous Mexican actors and even some rock concerts. The actors who performed on stage were Julio Aleman, Maria Velazco "La India Maria," Lorenzo de Monteclaro King Clave, Nelson Ned, Valentin Trujillo, Beatrice Adriana, Armando Almada and Jorge Lavat.

Along with my parents Jose J. and Ramona S. Marquez, my brother Perfecto and sisters Eva, Sylvia and Maria Elena as well as my cousins Elsa and Linda Marquez, the other staff members of our operation were:

Projectionists:

Guillermo Rodriquez, Jose Natera, Salvador Sanchez and Daniel Saldana

Food Concessionaires:

Maria Gloria, Rosa Gloria, Irene Ambriz, Refugia De Alba, Guadalupe De Alba, Teresa Sanchez, Lucia Marquez, Amelia Verduzco, Angie Verduzco, Rosemary Coria, Stephanie Espinoza, Stephanie, Julia and Hilda Parrilla, Elena De Alba and Rosa.

Security Personnel: Tony Hinostroza, Steve and Moises

I credit the Fox Theatre for my ability to buy my first home, meet my sweetheart at the Fox whom I ended up marrying, completing my college education and having the time to work closely with my family. I also gained a lifetime of great friends and the rare opportunity of experiencing the entertainment business where I can truly say, "There's no business like show business!"

Thanks for the memories,

— David Marquez, January 2005

Memories

I went to the "Thriller" fight as guest of Pepsi. When we were in high school from 1955 to 1959, I had a car in 1958 and drove to the show. My future wife, Janice and I, met other couples and our dates were done mostly at the Fox. I married her in 1961. I remembered the usherettes were very attractively dressed in slick bright colors and pill-type hats like the Philip Morris bellhop. The whole upstairs was filled with kids.

— Gary Podesto

We took a tour in 1979 when folks were trying to "Save The Fox" campaign. About 250 people took the tour with us.

— Del McComb

Chapter 8
Changing Venues

One would think there was a void in the history of the Fox California in the 1980s. Although first-class and even second-class movies no longer dominated the stage, the theater took on new roles: a place for charity events, entertainment, and home to the Hunter Square Acting Company. This period is best seen as the Merlo-Lawton era.

Edward Merlo, a local architect with a deep interest in historic structures, purchased one half of the Fox from Douglass Wilhoit, Sr. whose shares came from his two grandaunts Elsie Wilhoit Hodgkins and Mary Wilhoit Hodgkins. Madeleine Grunsky Lawton, of the pioneering Grunsky family, received her half from her Aunt Algae, wife of Eugene Wilhoit, and also from Arthur Wilhoit's granddaughters, the McKeever sisters.

The Merlo-Lawton combination, while seemingly an incongruous pairing of an elderly lady and a young architect, allowed each to work on different aspects of the theater. This partnership was to last for more than a decade and a half. Merlo, the preservationist, wanted to insure the historic integrity of the old theater. He saw himself as an architectural caretaker.

"…held a premiere night in January of 1981 spotlighting the film, Stockton, A Place to Remember.*"*

Madeliene Lawton seemed a feisty, tenacious, one-sided, no-nonsense octogenarian and very much an anomaly. She was quite misunderstood. For all the properties and stocks she received from her Aunt Algae, Lawton would easily have been recognized as one of Stockton's most affluent. Instead, this mother of three and married to Philip Lawton, an independent insurance man, continued to live in a small, unassuming bungalow on South Olive Street, east of Highway 99. Lawton was, in the words of her attorney, Dennis D. Geiger, "…frugal, typically unpretentious and, even after she inherited her wealth, she was comfortable and saw no need to move."

A careful study of six 12"x14", over 1-1/2" thick scrapbooks carefully detailed programs and activities at the Fox from 1980 to 1990. This vast collection of newspaper articles, flyers, announcements and letters amassed by Lawton's late daughter, Beverley, actually shows Lawton's persona. She was passionate about Stockton's downtown and more so about the theater. Lawton wanted it as a draw for downtown and did have preferences on the type of entertainment that would illuminate the graciousness of the theater. Yet, she kept an open mind and encouraged a variety of venues.

These two owners generously donated the theater for local and civic fundraisers, reunions, and even conferences. These organizations ran the gamut of Stockton's society. In April of 1980 the Stockton Public Library held its 100th anniversary in the lobby with reporter Mel Bennett autographing his newly-published *Stockton Theatres of Yesteryears*. The following month, as part of Stockton's Art Commission's Art Festival, the Fox celebrated three nights of 1930s films depicting the golden age of Hollywood: *Putting on the Ritz*, *Top Hat*, and *Alice Adams*. Those nights included patrons in period costumes, a tour and champagne. In the Fall a ten-member children's theater group presented *"Pirates of Penzance"* to benefit the building fund of St. Stephen's Church. This was followed by an Omega Nu Art Exhibition and Auction.

Carlon & Field Productions .....

ELVIN BISHOP!

Plus 2 Special Guests and Host Jim Kirk

50TH

Anniversary of Fox Theatre in...

STOCKTON

October 24, 1980

8.50 ADVCE.
9.50 D.O.S.
DOORS OPEN 7

Lawton Scrapbook

No report of this event could be found in the newspapers but this flyer acknowledges that the Fox did celebrate its fiftieth birthday.

The United Filipino Youth organization raised funds by showing *"Revenge of the Bushido Blade"* with movie star Cameron Mitchell and kung fu/local minister Leo Fong making personal appearances. Even the Stockton Convention and Visitors Bureau held a premiere night in January of 1981 spotlighting the film, *Stockton, a Place to Remember*, a 14-minute film intended to lure tourists and conventions to the city. The night included stretch limousines for the dignitaries, red carpet treatment, champagne reception and everything needed to mimic the tinsel and glitter of a Hollywood opening.

For $8.50 one lunched at the Fox on Italian chicken and ravioli and supported the San Joaquin County's District Attorney's Victim-Witness program. Jim Plunkett, the Los Angeles Raider quarterback, was the special guest for that event. Lincoln High School held a dinner dance in the rotunda and within a few short months Doug Wilhoit held his first fundraiser there when he ran in the San Joaquin Supervisor race. Victory Outreach sponsored the appearance of Nicky Cruz, an ex-gang leader turned author of four books. Cruz came to speak about his ministry. For this event he was given the moniker *Ex-New York Warlord*.

Nostalgia over their youthful days at the Fox was the impetus for Stagg High School reunion planners to select the theater for the twentieth reunion of the classes of 1965 and 1969. El Dorado Elementary School's gathering was far more inclusive incorporating the classes of 1916 to 1948. Celebrations included a wedding held on August 11, 1987, when Lori Genasci exchanged vows with Cris Rosales in a spectacular ceremony in the rotunda.

The Fox was not used primarily by an all-white society. There were minority groups who felt comfortable leasing the Fox, particularly those in the Filipino community. This may have been influenced by their going to the theater when the Marquez family ran Hispanic, Indian and Filipino films. The comedy review *Dolphy! Live!* with Dolphy Panchito and Alma Moreno appeared in November of 1986 and was sponsored by the Filipino-American Chamber of Commerce and the Maharlika Dance Troupe. Four months later the Filipino-American Chamber again sponsored another Filipino singer-movie star, Ace Vergel, and a quintet of comics, the *D'Crazy Corporation*.

Even though there had been a few disturbances on fight nights in the late 1970s, the Fox continued to host several more closed-circuit events knowing that such events were lucrative. One was a 15-round World Featherweight Title pitting Danny "Little Red" Lopez against Jose Caba, Salvador Sanchez versus Richard Rozelle and Ruben Castillo versus Negro Torres. Admission was only $10.00. A much more interesting and more costly fight ($20 admission) occurred in August of 1980 when Muhammed Ali Professional Sports presented the World Welterweight Championship between Jose (Pipino) Cuevas and Thomas (Hitman) Hearns telecast direct from the Joe Lewis Arena in Detroit, Michigan. Promoters had a difficult time building up an audience since neither contestants talked very much. Cuevas was defending his welterweight crown and the fight was labeled "World War II." (The Sugar Ray Leonard-Roberto Duran fight held in earlier months was billed as "World War I" and the winner was likely to get a shot at Duran.) Cuevas, at age twenty three, was nicknamed the "Mexican Butcher Boy" because his meat-cleaver fists earned him sufficient monies to buy a string of butcher shops. Hearns, the 21-year old from Detroit, went under the alias of "Motor City Hit Man" because "…he does his job quietly and then gets out of town." Cuevas was guaranteed $1.5 million and Hearns $500,000. Two other scheduled fights were on the same bill.

ON WITH THE SHOW

In 1981 Bill Barr, owner of Rock 'n Chair Productions of Modesto, signed on to promote the Fox. Barr, a former glass worker at Libbey-Owens Ford, was noted for his Mountain Aire Concert series. His vision for the Fox was to have rock, country, jazz and, even, Broadway plays. Barr wanted "...to model the Fox after San Francisco's Warfield Theater, another 'ancient' structure that had been resurrected and given a new profitable life." His enthusiasm was overwhelming and he estimated one million tickets would be sold the first year. To offset the fear of an unsafe downtown, he said management would spend $3,000 weekly to patrol the premises. He figured it would take $350,000 to spruce up the building which included repairing the roof and re-upholstering the seats. According to Eric Chennault, the foreman supervising the restoration:

This place is solid, all steel and plaster. It's one of the safest, most innovative entertainment structures of the '30s. The acoustics are perfect, not a dead spot anywhere. We've totally rewired – worked the first four days by flashlight. The old ventilation can't be improved on; air completely recirculates every few minutes through vents in the floor.

True to his word, Barr immediately booked teen idol Rick Springfield, heavy metal basher Cheap Trick, the Greg Kiln Band and several other rock groups. The June 1981, performance of Greg Kiln and his cult rock band, then known as one of the best in rock music, brought 738 in attendance. Jerry Garcia, formerly with the Grateful Dead, had just left his famous band and developed his new Solo Band. He was scheduled for an August 8, 1981 appearance. Garcia said, "...he's looking forward to the sound...and the silence of the 2,500 seat hall...music gets crowded in a club, but in a theater you can hear the silence." "It gives the music a pretty exposure that's as important as the music." As David Marquez and Ed Merlo's handyman, Brian Farnsworth, went about their chores, they each remember seeing Garcia on stage practicing and were impressed with his calmness and courtesy.

The New Year brought on larger crowds, perhaps many wanted to see the extensive renovations, but, more than likely it was because of the performers. On January 30, 1982, Emmylou Harris appeared with her renowned *HOTBAND* much to the appreciation of country western and pop aficionados. Harris said, "Someone told me this is the first time we've been to Stockton." She then asked, "How did we miss this place?" referring to the Fox "...a still beautiful, historic wonder of a building that seems particularly well-suited to her earthy evocation of American's

Courtesy of Mike DeLorenzo

The theater getting a little spruced up in 1981.

original musical genre." A news article by Tony Sauro estimated the crowd was 2,050. He indicated parking was not a problem and there was no incident. He commented "...it was a bit chilly inside but Emmylou and the beer-wine concession in the lobby balcony took care of that."

Two weeks later, *The Pretenders*, known for hard-rocking with the *Bow Wow Wow* "...a rock group not a dog act" played to 2,022 rockers. Vocalist Chrissie Hynde was "totally overpowering." The two encores showed that the audience was enthusiastic but not violent, even though people jumped up and down in the aisles. To Bill Barr, these two months' performances "…were an incredible success. I can't see it loosening up now or in the near future." In the month of March KZAP radio station sponsored the Huey Louis band that "wowed" 1,700 clapping and cheering fans.

May of 1982 was a busy month for the Fox. Leading off on May 1st was a well-advertised benefit for the University of the Pacific's Conservatory of Music Scholarship Fund and the Downtown Associates equipment fund. The venue was the 96-piece Oakland Symphony with young, Black conductor Calvin Simmons and Leland Lincoln as the soloist.

Lawton Scrapbook

Calvin Simmons, the brilliant young conductor of the Oakland Symphony, performed at the Fox in 1982. Unfortunately, he drowned at Lake Placid, New York, three months after his appearance in Stockton.

Simmons, at age 32, was well celebrated having been the conductor for the New York Philharmonic Orchestra, New York Metropolitan Symphony, Los Angeles Philharmonic Orchestra and the San Francisco Symphony. Simmons was not a stranger to Stockton for he previously conducted at Delta College's Atherton Auditorium in 1979. He departed from the traditional use of a baton as he felt his hands provided more guidance and communication with the musicians. Tickets, priced at $10.50 - $13.50, sold in many of the local outlets and nearby communities of Lodi, Manteca,

Modesto and Tracy. The only glitch was the refusal of the Stockton Arts Commission to endorse the event believing that it would compete with its own Stockton Symphony concert scheduled several days later. The Stockton City Council questioned the Commission's action as the group's mission was to promote art. One council member even threatened to reduce the funding earmarked to support the commission. Nevertheless, Simmons and the Oakland Symphony gave a flawless performance. Unfortunately, this young, gifted artist was to drown some three months later in Lake Placid, New York when he stood up in his canoe and it tipped over in the murky waters.

The venue changed dramatically when Joan Jett and the Blackhearts appeared on May 22nd. Barr claimed Jett would appeal to the teenagers. Jett "…is really hot now." Two nights later *Asia*, an all white male, progressive rock group took to the stage demonstrating the rock preferences of young adults. This back-to-back billing actually worked to promote Barr's own Mountain Aire Festival scheduled for June at the Calaveras County Fairgrounds. As many as 2,000 from as far away as Redding and Fresno converged in Stockton to see Jett perform a 90-minute show. Brian Kass, head usher said, "It was largely a teenage crowd that were well behaved – typical of recent rock concerts held here."

May finished with the *Primer Festival del DISCO DE ORO* on Saturday May 29th. Advertisement in Spanish for the Teatro Fox headlined eleven superstars of the Latin world such as Beatriz Adriana, Cruz Infante, Valentina Leyva and La Fronteriza with the Mariachi Azteca. According to reporter Tony Sauro, "Stockton's pop concert marketplace is overflowing in another direction, too.…" He was referring to the Hispanic market as an April performance of *Tierra*, a Latino funk and soul group, captured the joys of 2,000 people at the Civic Auditorium.

By summer, programs were few and far between with only the Pointer Sisters followed by Jethro Tull a few months later. December saw a return of Cheap Trick, and guitarist Rick Nielsen closed out the year. It seemed that the "rock" era at the Fox had run its course as evidenced by the return of Greg Kihn in January of 1983 that drew only a few hundred individuals.

The only major event in 1983 was Oakland Opera

Company's production of Verdi's *La Traviata* sponsored by the Stockton Opera Association. The Oakland Symphony and the Oakland Ballet dancers were also part of the program. Senior citizens, the handicapped and students in the Opera-in-the-School Program all received free tickets. Over a thousand attended of which 300 were children. The review was not flattering for opera star Susan McClelland in the lead role of Violetta Valery. The story line had the heroine fatally ill and, thus, ends the opera's romance. McClelland's performance was less than stellar for she was, indeed, under the weather and could not project the full richness the aria demanded. However, the *Stockton Record Editorial* did give kudos to the Stockton Opera Association and encouraged the organization to continue bringing more of this type of entertainment.

Unfortunately, grumblings began to surface indicating that the Fox had been turned over to the younger set. The Fox had provided a steady diet of rock and roll. While profitable, it was not helping make the theater a center for the performing arts. With Barr no longer on contract by late 1983, Madeliene Lawton and Edward Merlo reached a one-year agreement whereby she paid Merlo $100 a month to allow her to run the scheduling end of the business. Lawton was to do all the work and pay the expenses involved with the productions; then, she, solely, would reap the profits. The two of them, however, would continue to split both the rent receipts and bear the cost of maintaining the Fox and the adjoining commercial rentals. Even though it appeared that Merlo had a "hands off" role, this was not the case for he continued to assist in all of Lawton's endeavors.

Madeliene Lawton formed her own Lawton Productions in late 1983. Donald Bean of Offshore Productions from Fresno completed a feasibility report for Lawton in October of 1985, and agreed to serve as the director and general manager of the theater for one year at the salary of $3,000 per month. The contract stipulated:

Courtesy of Genevieve Lawton Sarabia

MADELEINE LAWTON and DONALD BEAN. Bean's Offshore Productions served as manager and booking agent for the Fox during the Merlo-Lawton era of the mid-1980s.

Such services, as production assistance, ushers, security, sound, lights, catering and box office services will be made available by Offshore to clients of the Fox Theater. Offshore shall bill these services directly to such clients and Mrs. Lawton shall assume no financial risk for these services. These same services shall be provided to Mrs. Lawton for the performances she chooses to promote at the same cost incurred by Offshore Productions.

Even though the theater had undergone major renovations four years prior, there were still problems with the fly system, rigging, electrical, heating, and cooling system which Bean insisted they fix immediately. The parties agreed that Fox would still be made available for civic, charitable and social organizations and set the commercial rental rate between $750 to $2,000 for the promoters.

Courtesy of Becky Lina Potten

Local charities, business events and reunions continued to take place at the Fox in-between booked performances.

Bean began to book events immediately starting with the *American Dance Machine* in October of 1985. This was a cast of twenty one dancers performing a variety of dance routines for an audience of twelve hundred. Dianne Runion concluded in her review, "…the audience left little doubt that Stockton is ready for some big city entertainment and that we are willing to go downtown to a theater that holds many happy memories for several generations of locals." The following month *Cotton Patch* came to town. Russell Leander starred in this national touring bluegrass, gospel musical. The story of the Magi was in a modified modern setting in the South with five actors playing multiple roles. Mike Fitzgerald ended his review by saying, "…what Offshore is bringing to the Fox deserves the attention of Stockton."

As Don Bean took to booking shows, he realized there was a "100-mile" dilemma that the theater faced. Stockton is caught in the one hundred mile radius between Sacramento and San Francisco and there is a ban against promoters booking appearances within the radius to those cities' theaters. It is the type of lock-in that damages attempts for a steady run of entertainment in Stockton. Bean thought of a two-pronged strategy: a) to assure the San Francisco booking agents that Stockton does not have the same audience as those in the city and, therefore, would not be in competition for attendance, and b) look to the Los Angeles market for the artists. Bean was sure Stockton would support jazz and wanted to target the 25-55 age group. To him, "It is a contrast to the teenage rock market of heavy metal funk and punk." Thus, for the 1986 schedule, Bean included a three-show jazz series sponsored by Michelob Beer.

Mid-January of 1986 began with the *Big Band Hit Parade Revue* with Carmen Cavarello, June Valli, Herb

Jeffries, balladeer from Duke Ellington's Orchestra, and the Gene Krupa Orchestra. Each was a showman in his own right. There were special prices for seniors and students. The ads also indicated that if one paid cash then they were guaranteed the best seats available.

On March 7th Spyro Gyra came to town. This seven-man jazz-fusion band was nominated for two 1986 Grammy Awards and was listed as the MCA Recording Artists #1 Jazz Group for 1985. A small amount of the profit was earmarked for KUOP, the

university's non-profit public radio station. Thirteen hundred turned out and as Barbara Abels said in the *Stockton Record* review, "Not even the winter rains could quench the fire of their Friday night concert.…" At the end of March the United States Air Force Band gave a free jazz concert that was sponsored by Downtown Stockton Associates and the *Stockton Record*. *The Crusaders*, another jazz group, came the following month.

Robert Guralnik brought his one-man show, *"Chopin Lives!"* to the Fox in early May. Similar to a Chautauqua, Guralnik introduced a new dimension of understanding about the Polish composer. One comment made in the next day's review was, "And to think that we once took buildings like this for granted. We know now that the Fox is a downtown treasure and good for Stockton for saving it.…" At the end of May two other major performances graced the stage.

George Carlin came on May 28th and gave a 90-minute performance to one thousand attendees. These were mostly the under 35-year old crowd. Two days later Arlo Guthrie and John Prine appeared in a three-hour concert with approximately the same number in attendance. Dianne Runion put in her review, "[Guthrie] looked like a latter-day hippie caught in a yuppie time warp." However, he got two standing ovations and the audience included the very young and senior citizens. This event raised more than $2,300 for the homeless shelter of which Bean served as one of the directors. It was Bean's idea of combining a concert and a fundraising campaign. Madeliene Lawton donated the theater, Lightswest the lights, Speeda Sound the sound equipment and the *Stockton Record* the advertising.

Wynton Marsalis and his quartet led off the Michelob Jazz Series in the month of June. Marsalis, a top trumpeter, had just been recognized as the Jazz Musician of the Year in 1985 in *Downbeat Magazine* and was also the 1984 Grammy winner in both the jazz and classical divisions. The following month the *Yellowjacket*, a group that played "fusion" or rock and jazz appeared. Although as famous as these performers were, the box office did poorly, both shows garnered less than six hundred people each night. One conjecture for the *Yellowjacket's* low turn out was that it was on a weeknight and the weather was extremely hot. In his column Stanley Klevan mused, "Stockton's spotty track record in greeting jazz greats might lead fans to worry about such music in the future here."

British power rock band, the UFO, came in August. There were two local boys in this band, Lincoln High graduate Tommy McClendon using the nom-du- rock Atomick Tommy M., and Lodi's Jake Johnson. George Thorogood, a blues guitarist accompanied by the Delaware Destroyers, was here after Labor Day. Local fan Gladys Racette wrote in the Letters to the Editor, "Stockton doesn't have much of a 'rock 'n roll' following, but for those of us who enjoy it, we

appreciate the efforts of the people who arranged everything."

In the Fall there were two shows that ran back to back with high attendance. On October 16th, *The Jets*, also known as the Wolfgramm kids, "set off thunderous applause and hysterical screaming from a crowd ranging in age from five to forty-five." This Mormon family, originally from Tonga, was now based in Minneapolis. The oldest eight children out of seventeen performed a 90-minute 14-song set that was good clean family entertainment much in keeping with the standards of the Mormon faith.

Jon Conlee appeared the following night and helped the Fox celebrate National Country Music Month in the Grand Ole Opry style. Local country-western radio station KFMR 100 sponsored the event. Conlee's performance is best described as having "down home" touches including slides of his ranch. The radio station

Lawton Scrapbook

Zasu Pitts Memorial Orchestra played to a near-capacity crowd in 1987.

sponsored a country dance competition at Hunter Square in conjunction with Conlee's performance.

Stanley Jordan, jazz guitarist, also appeared in October for the third in the Michelob Jazz Series. At this juncture even Bean acknowledged that "perhaps Stockton's economy was not really formatted for that kind of music." For a 2,500 seat house, Sypro Gyra drew the greatest audience at 1,300. Did Bean misjudge

Courtesy of Lori Genasci Rosales

The Fox marquee announcing the Rosales-Genasci Wedding.

the taste of the general population? One might consider that the term "jazz" refers to different types such as Fusion, Dixieland, or Rhythm & Blues. Those who appeared at the Fox may not have suited jazz aficionados of all ages. Bean was disappointed, he really loved jazz and thought others would agree.

Madeliene Lawton went all out on a special program during the Christmas season. The show, *California Country Music,* was a locally produced musical revue starring John Anderson. Although the crowd was fairly small, it was considered Lawton's "pride and joy." According to reporter Stanley Klevan, "…this takes the Fox into a new direction." He continued, "Since 1985-1986 the Fox put on 15-20 events with no incidents or problems downtown."

Courtesy of Lori Genasci Rosales

The spectacular Lori Genasci and Chris Rosales Wedding took place in the rotunda in August of 1987. To date this is the only wedding performed in the theater, although there have been other wedding receptions held there.

The 1987 schedule was rather eclectic. In early April the Zasu Pitts Memorial Orchestra, a 13-piece band, billed as San Francisco's hottest rhythm-and-blues band, played rock'n'roll classics from the 1950s and '60s. There was a near capacity crowd. It was popular because their style was a cross between the Blues Brothers and the showmanship of Manhattan Transfer. In mid-May Greg Allman appeared with his band sponsored by KDJK-FM and Tower Records. The program included a random drawing whereby thirty lucky winners won a four-hour cruise down the Delta with Allman. Their destination was Lost Isle and back. Allman's performance earned him a solid seven-minute chant for encores of which Allman obligated with two more songs.

The Jets returned a week after Allman but drew a smaller crowd than the previous year. The major complaint was that the program was an hour shorter and the ticket price was much higher. The Wolfgramm children had made a name for themselves in London and were on a grueling schedule of 66-cities tour in two months. By the time they reached Stockton, exhaustion had set in. One can read the frustration in Mitchel Koulouris' review while writing about the Jets he indicated "…the small crowd makes one wonder why Stockton doesn't seem to support shows at the Fox regardless of the act on tap." Koulouris continued:

The theater is an attractive, comfortable venue-possibly the most attractive and best sounding Stockton has to offer. Perhaps area residents don't realize the theater's importance or fail to see it as a serious attempt to bring quality entertainment to the city. How long will the facility promoters be able to operate given the apathy that greets them?

Other scheduled shows continued to see a dwindling audience. Sawyer Brown, a high-energy country music quintet drew only 400; and, even Jim Stafford a year later saw only 500 in attendance. Stafford, a television personality, comedian, banjo-guitarist and story teller, gave a "gut-splitting joyous entertainment." The opening act was Delta College alumnus Michael Corley on his 12-string guitar and was considered the best this side of Chicago.

With each show Lawton spent hundreds of dollars on advertisement and flyers and attempted to reach all facets of communication. She wrote letters, encouraged sponsorship, endorsements and made sure that the local newspapers not only ran her paid advertisements but also wrote previews as well as reviews. It did not matter

Courtesy of Jim Watson

These three photos are among a dozen taken to show the deteriorated state of the Fox just before it closed in 2000. Top: stage, middle: right balcony, and bottom: a look from the balcony into the projection booth windows.

who wrote the reviews, the reporters, themselves, often showed their frustrations at the lack of attendance. At the same time it was obvious they felt for Lawton and admired her tenacity.

In looking for the right venue, after two years of hard rock music followed by several years of jazz and then country music, the theater began to have its fair share of gospel music often sponsored by non-profit and church groups. The gospel duo Philip and Brenda Nicholas performed in April of 1987 and the following month the Dunham Brothers, a seven-member gospel singing group performed a *We Say No To Drugs* show that included the 60-voice Temple Baptist Choir of Lodi and the Triumph Family Gospel of Atwater. The booking calendar from 1987 to the end of the decade was frequently saturated with various other Christian music performers. They found the stage and the sound system at the Fox a good venue to deliver their message. It became very evident that the use of the Fox was opened to almost everyone and every faith. The last program before the Fox closed was in January of 1988 when Mylon Le Fevre and the Broken Heart Band played Christian music. Their tour across America program was entitled *Crack the Sky.*

Concurrent to the efforts of Rock 'n Chair Productions and later with Offshore Productions, Lawton also became the patroness of the Hunter Square Acting Company whose tenure at the Fox lasted about six years (1981-1987). By the closing years of the '80s decade it was apparent the owners had not found their market – or, perhaps Stockton, entertainment and society in general were changing too rapidly. Brian Farnsworth who worked for over twenty years as Edward Merlo's handyman said the business was tough and the theater's repair demands were constant. As the all-around building manager, he was the first on the site and the last to leave. Farnsworth really loved the building and worked hard at historic restoration. The demands of the visiting performers were often hard on the stage and its equipment. The main switch to all the light panels for the auditorium was up in the projection room. It was dark and eerie climbing that long flight of stairs guided only by a hand-held flashlight. He got the same spooky feeling when shutting down the outdated, antiquated and, often, broken down boiler in the basement.

The curtain did come down and the doors were locked at the Fox by late 1988. Other individuals made their way back into the theater not to perform but to establish residence. It was much easier and less visible going through the Market Street alley entrance. Aside from the sporadic homeless individuals, prostitutes also moved in. They rigged an almost undetectable wire that tripped the lock on the panic door. They, literally, helped themselves to everything and anything to make their stay in the dressing rooms comfortable. The set up housed at least three to four prostitutes. One day while Farnsworth was checking for roof leaks and the drainage system he noted that someone made holes in the door and the built-in safe on the first floor. They even absconded with his portable radio when he absentmindedly left it to do some repairs. Taking his assistant, Alvin Sibell, the two men cleared the living quarters. Fairly expensive clothes hung on hooks, velveteen sheets covered the mattresses and there were hot plates for cooking. They removed three large bags of clothes and donated them to the Cancer Society as well as a bicycle found inside the room and they dumped the syringes and other drug paraphernalia. Farnsworth then got a special permit to put bars and chains on the outside exits to prevent the prostitutes and anyone else from breaking in.

The Fox closed by 1989. It was a valiant struggle for Edward Merlo and Madeliene Lawton who together poured hundreds of thousands of dollars into the theater just to maintain the building and make it safe, if not always presentable. There were some very good shows but the draw was not enough to rescue the financial burden on the Merlo-Lawton partnership. Stockton was to see other start-and-stop efforts in the 1990s until the Fox was rescued through government intervention.

Sylvia Sun Minnick

Memories

Jamie Farr of M.A.S.H. came to Stockton to do a live production of the Odd Couple. There was a big fanfare for Farr who drove the Willie Jeep down Main Street. Productions at the Fox raised enormous money for various local charities.
— *Marian Jacobs*

Chapter 9
A Theater Within The Theater

Without a doubt, the Fox California's programs, events and attendance waxed and waned in the 1980s. Yet with all the attempts to make use of different venues in the main auditorium, co-owner Madeleine Lawton never diverted from her passion of making the Fox a center for performing arts. For almost six years, Lawton nurtured and generously donated the use of the theater to a local amateur acting group, the Hunter Square Acting Company (HSAC). Lawton knew Stockton's cultural heritage would be enhanced if HSAC and other forms of entertainment jointly and consistently utilized space in the vacant and badly dilapidated theater during its "down" period.

HSAC, formed as the result of a conflict which had apparently been brewing for some time between Stockton Civic Theater and its Artistic Committee, brought theatrical innovations to the community through productions at the Fox California. The Stockton Civic Theater (SCT) made front-page headlines on Saturday, December 17, 1980, with the announcement "Civic Theater trustees reject plays, panel." The Board of Trustees, SCT's governing body, made the decision that the services of the Artistic Committee were no longer required. Therefore, the entire nine-member committee was dismissed— Bill Grotemeyer, Ric Gauuan, Nick Elliott, Scott Hall, Susan Harloe, John Jutt, Nancy Kahn, Pat Manning, and Frank Jones, the individual who had formed the original company in 1951. The reasons were "complicated" but boiled down to "confusion in philosophy between the board and the Artistic Committee."

Undaunted by the dismissal, Scott Hall, a veteran of twenty years as an actor, director and technician with SCT, formed Hunter Square Acting Company, a non-profit, public benefit corporation, on July 14, 1981. Joining him in directing were Ric Gauuan, experienced actor and director who also had extensive experience as a set, costume, and lighting director, and Dorothy Mulvihill, actress, set and costume designer, director, long-time member of SCT, and drama director at Manteca High School.

Members of HSAC's Board of Directors were Ed Merlo, Madeleine Lawton, Max M. Carroll, Tim Cassidy, Bill Chapman, Ed Coy, Rudy Croce, R. M. Eberhardt, F. J. Dietrich IV, Don Geiger, Bernice Huston, Paul Jacobson, Marvin Marks, Greg McKeegan, Carl I. Peregoy, Bob Snyder, Thelma Stewart and Scott Hall. The production staff included Mulvihill, Gauuan, Jones and Judy Caruso Williamson.

Scott Hall indicated in an interview on August 11. 1981, "This is not a split-off group; the people helping us were very specific that they're not breaking their ties with SCT…. I think the community can support two community theaters."

Hall had every confidence that he could raise the funds necessary to support HSAC. He made the statement in an interview conducted in 1983, "I can get on the phone at any time and get help, now." He was flying in the face of the fact that the local community,

Courtesy of Dorothy Mulvihill

SCOTT HALL, in costume, for his role as Skip Hampton in the comedy-drama *Lu Ann Hampton Laverty Oberland* in 1982. Hall was the driving force behind the creation of the Hunter Square Acting Company.

as reported in 1978, was heavily invested in Stockton Civic Theater. SCT, which had been utilizing the Madison School auditorium for its productions, and later a location at Monroe and Willow Streets, was in the process of opening its own theater at Venetian Bridges on a $165,000 piece of property donated by Eckhard Schmitz. The project was near completion in 1981 when SCT dismissed the Artistic Committee.

In the meantime, Hall jumped into the creation of HSAC with both feet. His first step, although it is not clear just when he obtained permission, was to obtain a rent-free space at the Fox California. The next step was a fund-raising letter dated August 12, 1981. Another money-raising concept was the renting of the Fox marquee. One of the first to rent the space was Delta Lumber Co., and on September 5, 1981, the marquee read "Delta Lumber Co. Supports the Hunter Square Acting Company." These initial fund-raising efforts

netted $15,000—enough for Hall and a contingent of friends to begin converting an upstairs rent-free space at a badly deteriorated Fox California into a "little theater." Hall said, "I don't think the room had been used for 35 years. …It was full of pigeon crap. I wish we had a before and after picture. It was a mess. The room has a nice appeal to me. It has good acoustics." Hall and technical director Jack Pratt built over an ersatz fireplace but left the balance of the room as it was, "…including a vintage chandelier—in its original state. Portable lighting systems [were] installed—enabling them to leave the plaster ceilings and walls intact." However, the stage specifically constructed for the space left seating for a mere 66 people. It was indeed a little theater.

In November of 1981, everything was in place for the opening of HSAC's first production, *Artichoke*, a comedy/drama by Joanna M. Glass, described by the Christian Science Monitor as "a haunting play about coming to terms with life." It was directed by Ric Gauuan and featured Jim Hatton, Dick Pratt, Jenith Hall, Scott Hall, Robyn Fass, Frank Wilbur, and Mike Fitzgerald, columnist for The *Stockton Record*. All seats were sold out within thirty-six hours and two added performances were also sold out. Wrote The *Stockton Record*, "New theater group debuts with triumph." Not to minimize the production's success, but certainly curiosity and interest in just what had been done to the interior of the Fox California may have been the drawing card.

Next came *Buried Child* in February of 1982, a drama by Sam Shepard, a tale of the disintegration of the American Dream, directed by Ric Gauuan. Cast members were Marvin Marks, Dorothy Mulvihill, Scott Hall, Steve Stinnett, Ann Samuelson, Mike Wightman and Morgan Stewart. Again, the newspaper would proclaim, "Hunter Square company scores hit with 'Buried Child'."

In May 1982, *Christopher Robin, Pooh and Friends*, based on the works of A. A. Milne, was conceived, directed and costumed by Dorothy Mulvihill and performed on the Fox California's main stage by the Manteca Young Actors' Children's Theater. The production featured Melissa Johnson, Barbara Price, Robin Price, Kim Jager, Deanne Detmers, Andy Gouldh, Wendy Vosper, Penny Sampier, and LaVonne Burg. Parents and children were admitted free as HSAC's gift to the community.

Also staged in May 1982 was *Bleacher Bums*, conceived by Joe Mantegna, and written by Chicago's Organic Theater Company. It was described as "A Nine-Inning Comedy," about irrepressible, irreverent Chicago Cubs baseball fans at Chicago's Wrigley Field. Jack Pratt, assisted by Ric Gauuan, directed cast members John Ancheta, Rob Crawford, Elmer Rodriguez, "who stole the show," Donald Moseley, Mike Whiteman, Robin L'Hoir, Barbara Evens, John Jutt, Ric Gauuan and Jim Hatton. *Bleacher Bums* hit a home run and went on the road with five more performances at Hotel Leger in Mokelumne Hill.

Ending the 1982 season was *Lu Ann Hampton Laverty Oberlander*, a comedy/drama by Preston Jones, the telling portrait of a girl's life through womanhood in a small, backwater Texas town. The play featured Dorothy Mulvihill, who also directed the production, Kathi Diamant (of Channel 13), Michael Wightman, Scott Hall, Steve Roland, Edward Betz, retired dean of all-university programs at UOP, James Hatton, David Woodward, Mike Fitzgerald, Ray Gebbie and Judy Woodfill. The *Stockton Record's* theater critic observed, "Hunter Square produces another winner." "[T]he setting is part of the production's charm. The Fox Theater holds many nostalgic memories of the '50's for Stocktonians, and this play performed in the Fox turns back the clock 30 years."

By 1983, the owners of the Fox, Madeleine Lawton and Edward Merlo, had made over $250,000 worth of renovations to the Fox California in hopes of attracting major productions to the main stage. In February of that year, HSAC, themselves, launched a campaign to raise $6,000 to convert the Fox rotunda into a playhouse. Scott Hall reported that in only two weeks they had raised $3600, enough to authorize the use of green velvet for re-upholstering the seats. Subsequently, over a two-month period, the fund-raising campaign brought in a total of $13,000 in community and business donations In April of 1983, HSAC presented *Romantic Comedy* by Bernard Slade, the first production in the rotunda, and initiated the use of a new stage, the portability of which was to be tested in the production

of *Luther* in October that year. *Romantic Comedy* was directed by Dorothy Mulvihill and featured Michael Fitzgerald, Debbie Creighton, Lynne Britting, Judy Woodfill, J. Brian Griffith and Barbara Price. The *Stockton Record* critic on April 17, 1983, felt that the play was an "Uproarious 'Romantic Comedy' sure to please." She also made note of the fact that "because of the high ceilings and large space, the theater is, however, rather chilly."

DOROTHY MULVIHILL in her signature role as Emily Dickenson in *The Belle of Amherst*, a one-woman show in 1985. Mulvihill directed a number of the productions.

HSAC struggled on and resumed production in the rotunda in June 1983, with *Shel's People*, based on the writings of Shel Silverstein, directed by Dorothy Mulvihill. The cast was composed of members of Manteca Young Actors' Children's Theater—LaVonne

Burge, Barbara Price, Melissa Johnson, Wendy Vosper, Sherry Kemper, Jennifer Lilly, Andy Gould, Matt Ratto and Tim Ratto. The *Stockton Record* critic described the offering, as an "Hour of enchantment: call it Children's Theatre" and began her critique with a very revealing question: "What can anybody do with nine teen-agers, three books of poetry, a $250 budget and 35 listeners?" She observed that if that "anybody" was director Mulvihill, the "middleaged playgoer [would] laugh, cry, think and feel." Unfortunately, this review would highlight lack of funds and lack of attendance. This was the second and last production held in the rotunda—in addition to its having been described as "rather chilly," Mulvihill, in June 2005, recalled that she and Hall had agreed that the acoustics were "lousy."

In October 1983, Scott Hall starred in *Luther*, a play by John Osborne, dramatizing the life of Martin Luther. Hall would have preferred only to direct, but being unable to find local talent willing to perform, he took the starring role, and co-directed the production with Dorothy Mulvihill. This huge production, too large for the "little theater," was staged at Central Methodist Church. It co-starred John Jutt, Pastor Greg Flechtner of Immanuel Lutheran Church, Scott Hall, Marvin Marks, Arthur Carpenter, Pastor Thomas Hausch of Trinity Lutheran Church, Jim Hatton, Ed Betz, Morgan Stewart, Alan England, Mike Fitzgerald, Dennis Donald Geiger, Martha Caves, Doug Knispel, Dale Stocking, Ray Gebbie, George Chimiklis, Paul Glennon, Jr., Elmer Rodriguez, Wayne Bennett, Ralph Anderson, Steve Thumlert, Robert Buck, Max Carroll, Monroe Hess, Tim Cassidy, Paul Glennon, Jennifer Moseley, Michelle Moseley, Shannon Hall and Heath Glennon. In an interview run on September 11, 1983, Scott Hall said the play *"will wipe out Hunter Square's resources,"* and added that every production drained the company of its resources, *"but that audience support always brought in enough to support the next undertaking."*

Although the newspaper provided extensive coverage, the reviews were mixed. The *Record's* drama critic felt "Luther eludes players' grasp." On October 26, 1983, Bob Camden of the *Manteca News* said in his column, *In My Opinion,* "Besides Hall's portrayal of Luther, the cast as a whole gave competent performances…." In a letter to the editor of The *Stockton Record,* Frank Jones, a member of HSAC who could hardly be deemed completely objective, described it as "a treat for the mind, ear and eye."

The next production in late March 1984 was to be *Fifth of July*, a play with homosexual overtones. It was well into rehearsals, when ironically, Scott Hall, himself, now in a position to veto a selection and director, and mindful of Fox owner Madeleine Lawton's strong opinions over language and types of productions, made a "politically correct" decision. He canceled *Fifth of July* because he felt that it would not be supported by HSAC's backers and that there wasn't an audience for it in Stockton. Hall was quoted as saying, "I've offended a director and a group of actors. I did not intend to be malicious. When I'm given a choice between offending a cast and director as opposed to our contributors and audience, you know what choice I have to make…." The director and cast secured the use of a church hall and planned to do an independent production some weeks later.

By May 1984, the hopes of using the Fox rotunda, with space for double the number of seats as the upstairs area, had simply dissolved into thin air. HSAC returned upstairs to the "little theater." On May 20, 1984, the company staged *The Dining Room* by A. R. Gurney, Jr., directed by Dorothy Mulvihill and starring Edward Betz, Deanna Mulvihill, John Niemi, Elmer Rodriguez, Randy Thorns, Judy Caruso Williamson (recipient of Stockton Civic Theater's 1983 Best Actress Award) and Judy Woodfill. Fifty-nine different roles were successfully performed by the seven-member cast. The *Stockton Record's* theater critic deemed the play to be so enjoyable "that it makes the $5.00 admission price the best invitation to a dining room in town."

The 1984 season concluded in September with *The Sea Horse* by Edward J. Moore, directed by Ric Gauuan, and starring Hall and Mulvihill. Wrote the reviewer, "'The Sea Horse'—rough-and-tumble, sensitive love story." "…Mulvihill and Hall have worked together as friends and colleagues for many years, and they appear to be particularly attuned to each other's nuances. Their acting is completely natural…."

The 1985 season had an auspicious beginning on February 17 with *The Belle of Amherst* by William Luce, a dramatization of the life of poet, Emily Dickinson. Dorothy Mulvihill, directed by Greg Morales, gave her signature solo performance as Dickinson. Mulvihill had toured with this role in central California, and had also performed in San Francisco and in Mainz, West Germany, for the Army Theatre. The press wrote, "The greatest joy of this performance comes from the range of emotion which Mulvihill realizes through her interpretation of the play." Despite this glowing review, attendance was untypically low for a Mulvihill tour de force.

In May 1985, another children's production, *Here We Are!* took place at the Fox with material from *Magic Theater* and Shel Silverstein, directed by Dorothy Mulvihill. The cast included Andy Andris, Dana Ballard, Michelle Cortez, Denise Costa, Shannon Hall, Jennifer Harvey, Jill Harvey, Reynaldo Lopez, Robert Lopez, Andrea McDonough, Erin Mills, Teri Miraglio, Michelle Moseley, Erin Reid, Gina Simas and Earl Williamson.

The 1985 season ended with companion pieces, *Sister Mary Ignatius Explains It All For You* and *The Actor's Nightmare* by Christopher Durang, directed by Judy Caruso Williamson. The production starred Mark McClelland, Christine Souza Luis, Dorothy Mulvihill, Judy Woodfill and Bruce Jernigan. Wrote the reviewer, "Durang comedies: 1 weak, 1 strong." " …[The] two

comedies have opened the jugular veins of literature and organized religion at Hunter Square Acting Company, Fox Theater on Main Street, where the plays opened…to a standing room only audience." The plays prompted an op-ed piece entitled "Is it free speech or anti-Catholicism?"

Bell, Book and Candle, a comedy in three acts by John van Druten, opened the 1986 season. In the cast were Judy Woodfill, Philip Urie, Jill Heard, Elmer Rodriquez, and Edward Betz. The theme of the play was witchcraft, but The *Stockton Record* reviewer's headline was *"Hunter Square play not quite bewitching."* This headline was considered by the writer of a letter to the editor to be misleading and unsupportive of local talent because at the end of the review, the critic observed "Almost certainly the play will improve with further plays. It's well worth the time and money for its charm, laughter and universal appeal…"

This is an artist's concept of the rotunda as it would appear for use by the Hunter Square Acting Company when they moved their playhouse from the mezzanine level to the rotunda. The move was not practical and they returned to their original site.

Unfortunately, *Bell, Book and Candle* opened without its director, Dorothy Mulvihill, who had suffered a broken leg as the result of an automobile accident. She was sidelined for several months. During the same period, the demands on Scott Hall had increased substantially since the founding of the company in 1981. He was chief fund-raiser, set builder, actor, director, and public relations manager, in addition to his work as a branch manager for Bank of Stockton. HSAC became dormant and remained that way for about six months.

On October 26, 1986, a headline in The *Stockton Record* asked, "Hunter Square: Is it curtains? Idle troupe faces doubtful future." Scott Hall was described as the "overtaxed" founder. Questions arose as to his continued management of HSAC. He assured the interviewer that there would be another production in March of 1987 but did not reveal its name. In that same article, Al Muller, drama instructor and director at Delta College, speaking of Hall's management, commented that although HSAC appeared to be run by committee, it was not, and that was its strength as well as its weakness. "It is very difficult to run a theater by committee. It has to be a benign dictatorship. I think that's why it has some focus, and why it was successful in developing a particular style of contemporary theater and why it has some burnout."

The play promised for 1987 was the one-man production, *Vincent*, which opened on March 8, 1987. Hall directed and starred in the dual roles of Vincent and Theo van Gogh. Leonard Nimoy (Mr. Spock of Star Trek) created the play from over 500 letters exchanged between brothers Vincent, the artist, and Theo, the art dealer. There were some concerns that another one-man show would not do well because of the untypical non-attendance for *The Belle of Amherst* by Dorothy Mulvihill enthusiasts. These fears proved to be unfounded. "…The Hunter Square faithful pounced on first-night seats, making the show's opener a sell-out 10 days before curtain time…"

Nevertheless, the production may have been the straw that broke HSAC's back. Hall miscalculated the work and cost involved—there was the added burden of a $1,500 insurance premium to cover the use of 140 borrowed slides of van Gogh's paintings. Projected on a pair of screens behind the performer, these slides served as a backdrop. The projector made so much noise that Hall wound up building two special booths swathed in carpets and insulation batting. "It had turned into a monster, but I got rid of the distraction." The scheduled performances were sell-outs, and enabled two additional encores to take place on April 10 and 12.

Vincent was the last of Hunter Square Acting Company's productions although members of the company had high hopes of continuing on despite Hall's fatigue and his necessarily lessened commitment. It was, however, Madeleine Lawton's decision not to accept anyone but Scott Hall as the leader of HSAC. It appeared that Hall, within the HSAC group, may have been the only one who had a head for business. The other members, while passionate about acting, saw their participation more as an avocation rather than a profession for they were, after all, amateurs. There were other factors: HSAC's inconsistent number of productions through the years, ticket prices ranging from three to seven dollars, at most, and for only sixty-six seats, did not amount to much income—and even though the newspaper write-ups were positive, HSAC was not able to entice a full house for each and every production. In essence, HSAC was a financial liability to the overall expense of running and maintaining the Fox.

Sadly, and irrespective of all her altruistic, long-held intentions to make the Fox a center for performing arts, Madeliene Lawton had no choice but to bring down the final curtain on Hunter Square Acting Company, a theater within the theater.

Marian Vieira Stevenson

Chapter 10
The Enduring Gift

The Fox Theatre in the 80s could be characterized as a private redevelopment effort. A variety of promoters, either for profit or passion, sought to revive the theater as an entertainment center. Those efforts kept it alive, not a vigorous, robust existence, but alive nonetheless. It bounced in and out of consciousness. The theater was an asset but, how to take advantage of it?

Madeleine Lawton, through Lawton Productions, demonstrated that a willingness to underwrite productions and assume losses did not guarantee success. Something was missing. Private investment and promotion wasn't succeeding in bringing back large or consistent audiences.

Discussions continued between owners Lawton and Merlo as to what could be done to preserve this great theater. In the early 1990s, the San Joaquin County Arts Council approached the owners about potential uses for the theater. From the Arts Council, Julie Kramer, executive director, and Clayton Shotwell, president, created a Fox Theatre Task Force. The group started meeting in 1991 to explore various uses. Meetings were generally attended by a core group of committed Stockton arts activists: Al Muller, Bill Smith, Sand Kukuda and Carmen Fernandez, along with Julie Kramer and Clay Shotwell. The task force encouraged the active participation of Ed Merlo and Madeleine's representative, Don Geiger. The group also included a vital link to the City of Stockton with the membership of Deputy City Manager Lyn Krieger. One of the primary focuses of the task force was to examine other theater projects for potential redevelopment models which could be used in Stockton.

> *"One always knew the Fox was a historic and priceless part of downtown."*

The group generally met at the Alan Short Gallery, and the February 18, 1992, agenda is particularly interesting in hindsight. After reports by theater consultants and a review of completed projects, Lyn Krieger was to report on the potential use of redevelopment funds. A seed had been planted, which over the next three years would germinate and grow into full City of Stockton participation in the Fox.

The task force continued meeting through 1992. In addition to the overarching issues concerning the Fox, the Arts Council also worked toward some intermediate uses of the theater. It was the group's desire to use the Fox for a series of Brown Bag

Concerts, both in the theater as well as in adjoining Hunter Square. The concerts would occur once a week during the summer months. The relationship between the owners and the Arts Council suffered when they couldn't come to an agreement for cost-sharing which would be acceptable and affordable for both parties.

On January 14, 1992, The *Stockton Record* editorial spoke of the theater as being a "catalyst" for downtown:

"… The warehouse at 420 Weber Ave. and the theater at 242 E. Main St. may have a lot in common. They could become catalysts, each in its own area, for reinvigorating the central city.

"… The privately owned theater is drawing the attention of the San Joaquin County Arts Council. Its president, Clay Shotwell, hopes to build a coalition of local artists, businesses and government

Courtesy of Marian Jacobs

A *Night At The Fox* invitation included dinner, viewing of the locally-filmed, award-winning *All the King's Men* and was hosted by Janet Leigh. This fundraiser benefited Stockton Beautiful.

to renovate the theater and make it a center for art and culture.

"… Alfred H. Muller, the Delta College instructor whose ideas about the Fox prompted the Arts Council to begin its campaign, had an interesting observation: 'In other cities, redevelopment efforts have only succeeded where they created some sort of major arts and culture magnet.' "

Unable to reach enough economic and political mass, the discussion between the owners and the Arts Council broke off and the Fox returned to its pattern of occasional events. From 1992 to 1995, there was no systematic use or strategic plan to develop the theater.

What happened at the theater was more a product of who approached the owners. Lawton and Merlo had made both a major emotional and economic investment in the theater. It required constant attention, if not to preserve, then just to slow the deterioration that inevitably occurs in older facilities. There were just enough activities (such as the touring presentation of *Chorus Line* in 1993) to keep the Fox in public consciousness. Dianne Runion's review liked *Chorus*

Courtesy of Marian Jacobs

Jeanette Helen Morrison, (1927-2004), better known as Janet Leigh, supported many local causes since 1950. That year, Leigh and Eddie LeBaron, quarterback for the College of the Pacific (University of the Pacific) kicked off a March of Dimes Drive at the Fox. Since then and until her death, Leigh returned frequently to Stockton which she called her home.

The Record

Today

Past, present & FUTURE

Comics
TV Listi
Ann Lar
Today's
Area Di
Pet of tl

*Nearly 2,000 fans jam Stockton's
Fox California Theater to enjoy
The Tommy Dorsey Orchestra*

City of Stockton files

Under VenueTech Management, the City of Stockton's Redevelopment Department spearheaded a three-year program to use the Fox California as a means to attract people back downtown. In August 1995, in what was described as a "tryout," the Tommy Dorsey Orchestra performed at the theater before a crowd of 2,000.

Line but commented that "the problem was chiefly from three directions: staging limitations, lighting and sound shortcomings, and Cow Town production glitches." The product was good but the package needed refurbishment in major areas. Still, despite intermittent use, the Fox remained visible and attractive.

During the early 1990s, a final critical component was coming into place. For many years, both the citizens of Stockton as well as its politicians had given up on downtown. It might be studied but there was no fortitude to confront the problem and take action. With the election of city mayor Joan Darrah and a new city council, things began to change. Downtown community leaders expressed their concern about the plight of downtown Stockton and its lack of security. Without knowing where the dollars would come from, the City Council voted for additional police to start making downtown a safer place. That City Council, and all subsequent city councils, have made the revitalization of downtown Stockton a priority.

The focus on downtown – coupled with a commitment to invest real money and staff resources – opened the door to the solution that ultimately saved the Fox. The seed that was planted in the early meetings of the Arts Council's Fox Theatre Task Force broke ground. There was now a city council intent upon making a difference. It wanted to make a change not only in the perception of downtown but also a change that grows out of bricks and mortar and tangible programs.

In February of 1998, Lyn Krieger wrote Don Geiger on behalf of the City of Stockton on a potential new direction for the Fox:

I am interested in exploring with you, on behalf of the Stockton Redevelopment Agency, the possibility of entering a lease with the owners of the Fox Theatre. The idea would be to provide an opportunity to bring quality performing arts, similar to the Nite at the Fox and A Chorus Line to downtown Stockton. My thoughts now are to locate a professional manager who would integrate us into an existing series of "road shows" which might be sold on a subscription basis...

The realization that the Fox could be used for entertainment and that entertainment could be used for redevelopment would become a major cornerstone for council-mandated downtown revitalization. One always knew the Fox was a historic and priceless part of downtown. The community always knew that it wanted live entertainment and, despite the independent efforts of owners Lawton and Merlo and the Arts Council, knew for sure it couldn't do it alone. The partner needed was now present and willing to participate.

With Lyn Krieger's direction, negotiations began on creating a lease which would place the Fox at the center of the downtown revitalization effort. Working with Barbara Anderson of the City Attorney's office, a lease took shape over the next several months. In June of 1995, the City entered into a redevelopment lease for the Fox. The lease provided for an initial three-year term, with the City having the option to extend for an additional three-years. The lease was designed to allow

the City to operate the building with a minimal rent of $1,000 per year to be paid to the owners.

Maintenance of the theater was a large issue during negotiations and would become even larger after the lease was executed and the City started using the building. Normal wear and tear and routine maintenance was to be provided by the City. Major repairs up to $4,000 for any specific operating system were to be paid by the landlord. Amounts above $4,000 were to be subject to further negotiations. The owners did not want to be burdened with major capital expenditures when they were not receiving income. The City did not want to commit to making major repairs on a building it did not own. This fundamental conflict would lead both parties to seek a different solution five years later.

Now that the City had the Fox as a redevelopment tool, it needed a plan for its use. The Redevelopment Agency issued a request for proposals for potential operators. The successful proposal accepted by the Agency was submitted by VenueTech, a Napa-based theater management company. VenueTech began managing the facility in September of 1996. The concept contained in the business plan submitted by VenueTech was to build community support for the theater by producing a series of shows which could be marketed as a package. Patrons could purchase tickets to the "Spring Series" or "Fall Series" and be assured of having their same seats for each show.

Prior to the first series, the Fox was "reopened" with a New Year's Eve performance by Ray Charles. It was a big event and it marked the return of big-name entertainment to downtown Stockton on a regular basis. Over 1200 tickets were sold for the show and many took advantage of the "Black Tie Option" to don their tuxedos. Ticket prices ranged from $65 to $85 and included champagne and hors d'oeuvres. Ray Charles counted down the New Year and really opened the new era of the Fox.

When the City leased the theater, it knew that community support would be vital to its success. To develop that support, Lyn Krieger, Don Geiger, John Bevanda and Leslie Crow began meeting in the summer of 1995 to discuss the formation of a new non-profit organization to support the Fox. From those early discussions came the creation of the Friends of the Fox Theatre, a 501(c)(3) not-for-profit that would provide community input both to the City and VenueTech on theater operations, assist in marketing the Fox, sell memberships, and encourage ticket sales. The first board of directors consisted of John Bevanda, Robin Burror, Leslie Crow, Don Geiger, Judy Johnson, Bonnie Mansfield, Carrie Sass and Jane Butterfield.

The Friends of the Fox Theatre, along with another new organization, the Downtown Stockton Alliance, worked to make the Fox visible to the entire community. The successful reopening was followed by the Spring Series, which consisted of *Diane Schuur* and *Count Basie, Blood, Sweat and Tears*, the *Smothers Brothers* and *the Lettermen*, *Bobby McFerrin*, the *Odd Couple, Grover Washington, Jr., Marvyn Hamlisch, Hiroshima*, and *Natalie Cole*.

The pattern had been selected for the next several years. VenueTech continued to book shows at the Fox and community awareness and participation grew over time. The arrangement with VenueTech (as did the lease with the owners) contained elements which would lead to the ultimate reexamination of the City's role at the Fox.

From the City of Stockton, California, Fall 1995

CityScape

Foxy Old Lady

City of Stockton files

Based on the success of the Tommy Dorsey show, preparations began in earnest for the reopening of the theater. The Fall 1995 issue of *CityScape* covered the details of all the clean-up preparations.

VenueTech was a management company. It was not dependent upon making the theater profitable. That may have been a goal but if not met, the City would ultimately underwrite losses. While the show series continued to draw patrons, there were not enough shows or enough diversity of shows to draw a new and expanding audience. The theater needed activity on a constant and ongoing basis with a broad variety of performances. The City was limited in the risk it wanted to assume, and VenueTech was unsuccessful in developing independent producers who would assume the risk for new shows' success.

VenueTech continued to book the tried and true (and some would say *tired* and true) as they were safe and appealed to the demographics, that the City had initially targeted as potential supporters of renewal. Those demographics needed to expand if the Fox was to be truly successful, and it did not.

The City Council and newly-elected mayor Gary Podesto began to become increasingly anxious to stem the flow of red ink and began to have reservations about the city's role as deep pocket producer of Fox shows. The economic losses only heightened the need to come up with a new model for the operation. The other

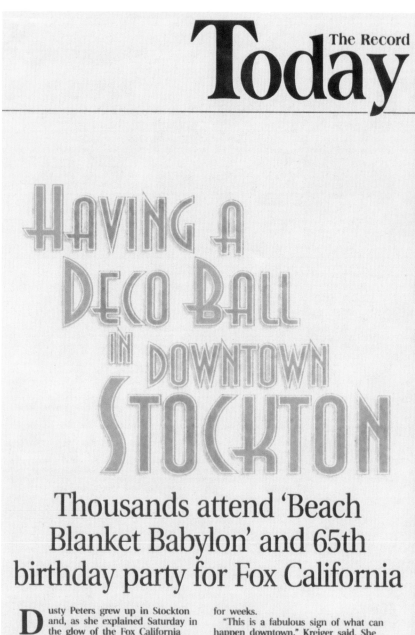

Today
The Record

Thousands attend 'Beach Blanket Babylon' and 65th birthday party for Fox California

D usty Peters grew up in Stockton and, as she explained Saturday in the glow of the Fox California marquee, attended Stagg High School in the late 1960s. "When I was in high school," Peters recalled, "we'd cruise up and down Pacific Avenue."

Peters left Stockton in 1969 and did not return until 1½ years ago. When she did, she took husband Tyler around town to show him her old haunts, only to discover that most of them had disappeared.

Peters counted the Fox California Theatre among the missing until Saturday night, when she attended Downtown Stockton's Deco Ball. The event drew thousands to the city's center to celebrate both the 65th anniversary

for weeks.

"This is a fabulous sign of what can happen downtown," Kreiger said. She added the Redevelopment Agency hopes to hire a manager/promoter for the Fox California by year's end.

Downtown Stockton's Deco Ball was sponsored by the Stockton-San Joaquin Convention and Visitors Bureau. The event transformed Hunter Square and Main Street, as the normally staid thoroughfare hosted hundreds of couples who spent the evening dining and dancing.

It was all carried out under the watchful gaze of Stockton police officers. Many in attendance noted the police presence was vital to the success of future events at the Fox California.

Courtesy of Mike DeLorenzo

The Stockton Record described *Beach Blanket Babylon* as a huge success when it appeared on October 14, 1995. This gave Stocktonians hope that this reincarnation of the theater would give it a new, long life. It took almost another decade before this hope became a reality.

impetus for a fresh look was the relationship between the City and the Fox owners. The conflict inherent in the lease was becoming a larger issue. With age and increased usage, more and more systems required repair and outright replacement.

The initial three years was about to expire on the lease. The City wanted to redefine the relationship and obligations before it committed to another three years; so in May of 1998, the owners and the City agreed to a one-year extension to allow them to continue to discuss a new relationship which would acknowledge the need for major repairs at the theater.

The initial lease discussions centered around the concept of a much longer leasehold term. The owners desired to shift the economic burden of all maintenance and repairs to the City, while the City wanted a long enough term to recoup its expenses. Once again, the rent was more symbolic than real, a base rent of $1,000 a year with a percentage rent to the owners only after the City had recovered all of its expenses. The parties centered on a twenty five-year term with two five-year options. That term, it was hoped, would allow the City to recoup any capital investment it elected to make.

The potential for major expenses was large and largely incalculable. As the City examined building systems, American Disability Act compliance requirements, and fire and theater systems, it began to question the advisability of a long-term lease. The owners, now the families of both Madeleine Lawton and Ed Merlo, were concerned with the length of the lease and the lack of any real commitment by the City to make repairs. The City could make the capital repairs that all parties believed would be ultimately necessary.

Increasingly, the City thought more of becoming the owner with complete control of the theater revitalization.

Time was becoming a factor as shows continued to be booked into the future. The extended lease term was about to expire, and the owners agreed to a second one-year extension to allow negotiations to continue.

Discussions between the owners and the City were

becoming more tense as frustrations on both sides rose with the inability to reach agreement. The City, through its representatives, started talking about the possibility of condemnation. The owners felt they were victims of their own success, having preserved the theater at great personal expense and, indeed, from possible demolition by the very City that now sought to acquire it. What was the Fox worth? Was it a white elephant or was it the crown jewel of redevelopment, a priceless piece of Stockton's history that could never be duplicated? Would the Fox become the battleground for lawyers and appraisers as each side sought to maximize its position?

The ultimate solution to the conflict lay in the family culture created by both Madeleine Lawton and Ed Merlo. Even though both were now deceased, the very motives which directed and guided their efforts in the preservation of the Fox had been instilled in both families. Both continued to view the preservation of the Fox as a worthy goal that transcended generations. Each family had slightly different internal priorities, but those priorities could be satisfied and the larger goal met. After careful study, examination and analysis, both families chose to gift their interest in the Fox to the City of Stockton, a gift for all generations. The historic architecture of the theater would be restored, preserved and returned to downtown Stockton by way of a gift deed which required that the building continue to be used for theater purposes. The plaque placed in the theater lobby after its rededication says it best:

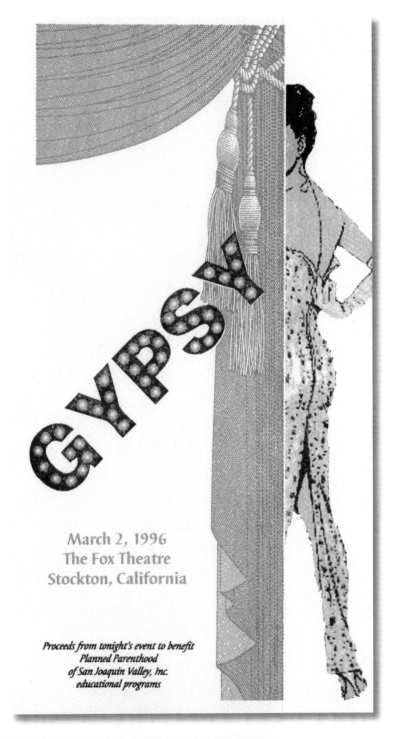

GYPSY

March 2, 1996
The Fox Theatre
Stockton, California

Proceeds from tonight's event to benefit
Planned Parenthood
of San Joaquin Valley, Inc.
educational programs

THE EFFORTS OF MADELEINE LAWTON, PRESERVATIONIST,
AND EDWARD CHARLES MERLO, ARCHITECT,
CO-OWNERS OF THE FOX
PRESERVED THE THEATER FOR FUTURE GENERATIONS
AND HONORING THEIR EFFORTS
THIS HISTORIC STRUCTURE WAS DONATED BY THEIR FAMILIES
TO THE CITY OF STOCKTON ON NOVEMBER 24, 1999

BEVERLY LAWTON   ANITA MERLO
GENEVIEVE SARABIA THE MERLO BUILDING TRUST
CHARLES MCCLEAVE

Don Geiger

Memories

The electricity downtown couldn't handle the street lights planned for the Beach, Blanket Babylon *gala and everyone pulled in generators and then we had to camouflage the generators. There were people up in the trees stringing up the lights on Main Street and Hunter Square. When the City was negotiating with the owners, someone said to me, "Are you Crazy? No one is going to come down there." Congratulations everyone.*
— *Lyn Krieger*

It was an amazing night. For the first time in many, many years, many even decades, that that many people were downtown late in the evening dancing in the streets with no worries. I went home around 2 or 3 A.M.; I had to unplug the lights from the generators.
— *Greg Folsom*

Chapter 11
Remembering Bob Hope

*I*t is remarkable that Stockton should be the first city in America to name
a theater in honor of Bob Hope, described at his passing at age 100 in 2003 as
"The World's Greatest Entertainer." In fact, the only other theater to bear his name is
not a movie house, but a little theater he adopted in his birth town of Eltham, England.

Courtesy of the City Clerk's Office

Bob Hope's daughter, Linda Hope, addresses the Stockton City Council after
a resolution changed the Fox California's name officially to the BOB HOPE
THEATRE. Looking on behind Ms. Hope are Alex and Faye Spanos and Hope's
son, Richard Hope.

It is not that Hope's contributions to entertainment, charity and his country
were ignored. The Guinness Book of Records declares he is the most decorated
entertainer in the world and the most honored and decorated American. His more
than 2,000 awards and citations include fifty six honorary doctorates, an honorary
knighthood from Elizabeth II, The Medal of Freedom by President Johnson,
Congressional Gold Medal by President Kennedy, and hundreds more.

The scope of the awards is an awesome tribute in itself. The entertainment citations reflect his mastery of stage, radio, television and movies. His humanitarian awards recognize his singular devotion to USO shows and entertaining service men and women at home and abroad for over fifty years (which garnered him the title of Honorary Veteran by unanimous act of Congress). His significant contributions to a huge number of other humanitarian causes are recognized again and again. Perhaps unexpected, there is a hefty sprinkling of sports awards, most in tribute to his promotion of golf. Worth special mention is a silver cup awarded by *Sports Illustrated* magazine on the occasion of his fifth hole-in-one (and he added two more!).

Lesley Towns Hope was born in Eltham, England in 1903, the fifth of seven sons. His father was a stonemason and his mother an aspiring concert singer. In 1907 the family immigrated to Cleveland, Ohio. In 1920 his father was granted U.S. citizenship, thereby making Bob and his brothers automatic Americans (though there was never a doubt that Bob Hope was *all* American!). Young Leslie Hope was a good athlete who fought nine bouts as a boxer. He was also a natural dancer and began taking lessons from entertainer King Rastus and Hoofer Johnny Root.

At age eighteen Hope and his girlfriend created a dance act that was successful in local vaudeville. At about this time he changed his name first to Lester and finally to Bob. He teamed with one partner and then another to modest vaudeville success before becoming a "single." In 1932 he made Broadway again in "Ballyhoo" and then found critical and public recognition in "Roberta." He went on to "Say When" in 1934 followed by the 1936 edition of the "Ziegfeld Follies" with Fanny Brice, and "Red, Hot, and Blue" with Ethel Merman and Jimmy Durante. He began making radio appearances early and in 1937 signed a twenty-six week radio contract for the "Woodbury Soap Show." In quick order he moved to Hollywood to appear in the movie, "The Big Broadcast of 1938" and to sign on with Pepsodent for his own NBC network radio comedy show. His radio show quickly jumped to number one with listeners. Throughout the years of W.W. II and on through the forties, America reserved Tuesday night for the blockbuster trio of comedy shows "Fibber McGee and Molly," followed by Bob Hope and concluding with "The Red Skelton Show." Radio success brought him almost instant national name recognition, which in turn, boosted his movie

career. His award winning radio show continued in popularity until 1956.

Vaudeville and Broadway reviews had allowed Hope to hone and refine his remarkable stage presence and timing and to define his comedic personae through repetition. But, a weekly radio comedy show demands a constant supply of fresh material. Hope met the need with his famous stable of writers. Reputed to be a tough boss by some, he, nevertheless, willingly gave them credit for their work and they were loyal.

Hope's movie career grew simultaneously with his radio popularity. Following his appearance in "The Big

Jerry Sola Collection

From the 1942 movie
The Road to Morocco.

Broadcast of 1938," he starred in several movies before the hit "Cat and the Canary" in 1939 with Paulette Goddard. "The Road to Singapore" in 1940 with Bing Crosby and Dorothy Lamour began a Hope-Crosby dynasty of sorts that would endure throughout both their careers. The picture was so successful that it resulted in a total of seven "Road" pictures (Singapore 1940, Zanzibar 1941, Morocco 1942, Utopia 1945, Rio 1948, Bali 1953, and Hong Kong 1962), a record for sequels that would stand until the "Bond, James Bond" series. *Time Magazine* described the Road pictures as "…rummage sales of stuff out of vaudeville, burlesque marvelously shoddy masterpieces of farce and fantasy, stitched together with clichés and ad libs."

The success of the "Road" series is often ascribed to the chemistry (read good natured rivalry) between the two stars. Crosby was even better known than Hope at the beginning; so the combination of the number one radio comic with the most popular crooner (who also had a popular radio show) had a synergy that promoted the careers of both, as well as their movies. The "Road" movies cast Crosby as the nonchalant, smooth con artist

A short list of his best remembered films over his long career would begin with "The Big Broadcast of 1938" with Shirley Ross and their bitter-sweet rendition of "Thanks For The Memories" which won the Academy Award for Best Song and gave Hope his theme song. The list would surely include "The Cat And The Canary" with Paulette Goddard in 1939, "The Princess And The Pirate" in 1944 with Virginia Mayo, Walter Brennan, and W.C. Fields, "The Road to Utopia" in 1946 (generally considered the best of the Road series), "The Paleface" in 1948 with Jane Russell in which he sang "Buttons And Bows," also an Academy Award

From the 1948 comedy *The Paleface* with Hope and Jane Russell.

From the 1938 movie *Thanks for the Memories*, the theme song became Hope's signature song.

and Hope as an inept braggart and likeable coward – a persona that would become his movie trademark as opposed to his "joke, joke, joke" stand-up act of "mildly irreverent" humor.

From 1941 through 1953 Hope's movies were annually listed in the top ten box office attractions in the country and he was declared the Number One box office attraction in 1949. He eventually made fifty feature movies and appeared in at least fifteen other films.

winning song, (and, until "Blazing Saddles," "Paleface" was the highest grossing Western spoof of all time), "Fancy Pants" in 1950 with Lucille Ball, "The Lemon Drop Kid" in 1951 with Marilyn Maxwell in which they introduced the holiday favorite song "Silver Bells," "Son of Paleface in 1952," (again with Jane Russell) considered a worthy sequel and remembered for the hilarious contributions of Roy Rogers and his horse, Trigger.

Two of Bob's later efforts of special note are "The Seven Little Foys" in 1955 that included a tap dance with James Cagney reprising his earlier award winning role as George M. Cohan, and "Beau James" in 1957, a film biography of New York's "slightly corrupt" mayor and king of Tammany Hall.

The roles he played were not conducive to Academy Awards, but his work was recognized and honored by

Courtesy of Hope Enterprises

the Academy with five separate honorary Oscars and awards. He also has four Stars on Hollywood's Walk of Fame. Hope was host or co-host to the annual Academy Awards telecast for a record seventeen years, beginning in 1960.

Bob Hope is not often credited as a singer, but he should be remembered for the songs he introduced that have since become standards. His Broadway debuts include "I Can't Get Started With You" and Cole Porter's "It's De-Lovely," a duet with Ethel Merman. Familiar songs from his long movie career include

"Thanks For The Memories," which became his theme song, "Two Sleepy People," "You Do Something To Me," "Buttons And Bows," and the perennial holiday favorite, "Silver Bells." In later years he adopted "Silver Bells" as the closing number for his shows, sung as a duet with a guest star or his wife, Dolores.

A quick decision to do a remote broadcast of his radio show for the airmen at March Field, California in May of 1941 – nine months before Pearl Harbor – resulted in another significant change in his career. The enthusiastic – almost overwhelming – acceptance of his show stunned Hope. Until that moment, he had not recognized how lonely and homesick the young troops were and how they hungered for entertainment and reminders of home.

The result was that with only nine exceptions, all of Hope's 144 W.W. II radio episodes were broadcast from a military installation either here or abroad. His first appearance in Stockton was on October 17, 1944, when his radio show was aired from Stockton Field, then an Army Air Corps flight training school. He had found a calling. The hallmark of the remainder of his long career would be his intense devotion to entertaining America's military personnel – wherever they were.

There was another aspect to this decision. All performers are at their best before an appreciative audience and the old vaudeville trouper quickly recognized this advantage. The enthusiastic reaction of the audiences also enhanced the broadcasts and, in a way, conditioned future audiences in what to expect at a Bob Hope show.

Hope assembled a small traveling troupe in 1942 to entertain troops in Alaska and the Aleutian Islands. This was the first in an annual series of USO trips abroad that continued until the end of the war. These included all of Europe, North Africa and Iceland as well as the Pacific Theater. His 1944 South Pacific tour traveled 30,000 miles and included 150 performances.

Peace was short-lived and the tours began again with the advent of the Cold War, beginning with the Berlin Airlift in 1948 and continued until his last USO appearances in Saudi Arabia, England, Germany and Russia in 1990. (Bob Hope was then eighty seven years old.) By 1953 Hope had entertained an estimated one million service people in over 400 camps, naval stations, and military hospitals around the world. Forty years later the number of people entertained would jump to 10,000,000. He made 700 trips to entertain military personnel.

The year 1948 began his tradition of USO Christmas shows that continued until 1990. The 1954 show in Thule, Greenland was filmed and televised as a special. It was so successful he continued to air them annually.

The early USO tours were often hectic, uncomfortable, strenuous and not without occasional danger (not to be compared with the conditions endured by the troops, of course). In W.W. II, Hope tried to schedule his shows as close to the front as possible (often within hearing of gunfire), but in Viet Nam when it was learned Hope was the target of a sniper and a possible hotel bombing, the military directed he perform only in secure locations.

His USO troupes grew in size as the years passed. The shows followed a formula that included Hope's monologue, sketches, music, and pretty girls. Some of the entertainers who accompanied him in

the early years included Frances Langford, Jerry Colona, Clark Gable (before he enlisted), Tony Romano, Bing Crosby, Fred Astaire, Dolores Hope, Jimmy Wakeley, Doris Day, Gloria DeHaven, Jinx Falkenburg and nearly always a current beauty queen. The 1948 Berlin Airlift show also included Vice President Alben Barkley, Irving Berlin, Elmer Davis, Gen. Jimmy Doolittle, and AF Secretary Stuart Symington.

Stars and personalities that joined his later shows included The Nicholas Brothers, Anita Ekberg, Margaret Whiting, Ginger Rogers, Hedda Hopper, Mickey Mantle, Jayne Mansfield, Gina Lollobrigida, Randy Sparks, Zsa Zsa Gabor, Steve McQueen, Andy Williams, Raquel Welch, Rosey Grier, Neil Armstrong, Redd Foxx and the list goes on, all worthy of mention. Either Skinnay Ennis or Les Brown provided music.

Alex Spanos (left) and Bob Hope in a dance routine for a charity event.

Hope would always strive to bring the best to "his boys." In the early years he managed to accomplish this while still hosting his weekly radio shows, making hospital tours, appearances at War Bond rallies and starring in movies. Later he would be free of radio, but still maintaining his movie and his television career and a heavy schedule of personal appearances.

The fifties inaugurated network television, a new entertainment venue even more challenging than the talking movie revolution. The early successes in network television were variety shows reminiscent of vaudeville. Hope called these shows "vaudeville in a box". Ed Wynne, Eddie Cantor, Sid Caesar, Milton Berle, and Ed Sullivan represented some of the more successful performers in this genre. Bob Hope refused a weekly variety series, fearing they would get stale in time. Instead he opted for monthly specials. After his first series of specials, he joined "The Colgate Comedy Hour" series by presenting "The Bob Hope Show" once a month. Later he joined "Bob Hope Presents The Chrysler Theater" introducing the show three weeks each month and performing in his own show the fourth week. After 1967 he presented only specials until 1997 when he was ninety four years old. In all he presented 284 NBC Specials over a period of forty three years that averaged, as whole, a whopping forty Nielsen audience share. His 1970 Christmas Special had the highest rating to that date and is still rated in the top fifteen of all-time. Critic Richard Corliss said he was "unquestionably the highest rated star in television history."

Golf was an important aspect of Hope's career. He was a fanatic. He played whenever he could, wherever he was. He took lessons from golf icon, Ben Hogan and at his best had a respectable handicap of four, good enough to allow him to be a participant in pro-am, celebrity, and charity tournaments. In 1965, the Palm Springs Desert Classic became the Bob Hope Chrysler Classic and Hope made it the premier celebrity golf event in the country. Over the years it has raised over $37,000,000 for charity and currently averages an annual donation of $1,500,000 to local causes, and it has become a model for other charity tournaments.

Bob Hope had begun to regularly use his celebrity status to raise funds for charitable causes during W.W. II when he teamed with fellow golf addict Bing Crosby in a series of exhibitions and tournaments on behalf of the American Red Cross. In his later years, after his movie and TV career waned (except for the occasional TV special), he continued a punishing schedule of over 200 personal appearances each year, mostly in charity events, auditoriums, colleges, and, of course, celebrity golf tournaments. During this period he raised funds for a broad spectrum of humanitarian causes, which explains, in part, why he was so richly honored and admired. It is estimated that the final total of his performing efforts and his own generous donations exceeds an astounding one billion dollars. He once told his friend, Alex Spanos, "If you don't have charity in your heart, you have the worst sort of heart trouble." Bob Hope lived by his credo.

He was a tireless promoter of golf. He habitually carried a golf club on stage when he was performing and often included golf scenes in his movies. He played golf with six presidents with resulting high profile news coverage. He used his celebrity status to encourage generals, politicians and show business stars to participate in charity tournaments. His golf book, "Confessions of a Hooker," was on the NY Times bestseller list for over one year, all of which led to his being installed in the Golf Hall of Fame. The citation that accompanied a gold medal awarded him by the PGA said in part, "one of the three people who have done the most for golf."

Golf was not Hope's sole sports interest. A real sports fan, the former boxer at one time owned minority interests in both the professional Los Angeles Rams football team and the Cleveland Indians baseball team.

At the 1969 tournament in Palm Springs, Hope found himself paired with another golf addict, Alex Spanos of Stockton, in a match against Bing Crosby and a friend. Hope and Spanos won the match, which so delighted Hope, he invited Spanos to continue as an occasional golf partner. Spanos was the country's largest builder of apartments at the time and the two successful sons of immigrant families found they had a lot in common, in addition to golf. They even improvised a short song and dance act and performed it at benefits throughout the world. The two families soon became very close and the Hope family became occasional visitors to Stockton as houseguests of the Spanos family. This friendship was the impetus that resulted in the naming of Stockton's rejuvenated movie palace "The Bob Hope Theater."

Dolores Hope is an integral and very special part of the Bob Hope story. Dolores Reade was a successful supper club singer in New York when they met and married in 1934, a marriage that would endure for sixty nine years. They performed together for a short time until they moved to California and adopted the first of their four children. At this point she gave up performing to devote full time to rearing her young family. This was not always easy since Hope was eternally on the road and therefore not always the ideal husband.

In the 1940's Dolores returned to the stage as part of Bob's USO shows. She was so well received she soon became a regular on his later tours. On their trip to Saudi Arabia in 1991 to entertain the troops of Desert Storm, she was the only female allowed to perform. She made eighteen guest appearances on Hope's TV specials. In the 1990's she resumed performing on her own and made several successful record albums.

In addition to being a successful wife, mother,

Courtesy of the Spanos Corporation

Two old friends enjoying each other.

grandmother, hostess, and entertainer, Dolores also devotes her time and talents to charity and good works. Some of the many official recognitions in Bob's collection were actually joint awards, recognizing Dolores' generous commitments to charity. She also owns a number of recognitions and awards for her good works.

It must be noted that Dolores Hope is also a pretty

good golfer. A cherished memory is the occasion when she and Bob played in a couples tournament in Palm Springs. After they completed their round, the loud speaker roared for all to hear: "Bob Hope seventy-eight, Dolores Hope seventy-six."

One of Dolores Hope's official biographies describes her well: "She's wife and mother; singer and sage;

homemaker; chairman of the board – a recording artist; and her golf game isn't bad either." She has her own star on Hollywood's Walk of Fame. Perfect.

Bob Hope was a phenomenon of colossal proportions and his career and achievements have been grandly recognized. There remains one more appropriate memorial to the great entertainer, patriot, and humanitarian. Bob Hope always remained a hoofer at heart. What is more fitting than placing his name in lights permanently on a grand theater marquee?

It is Stockton's privilege.

Robert Shellenberger

The City called and asked for help to finish the theater. They were willing to name it after me. That night I went home and talked with Faye. Bob and I have been the best of friends; we've traveled the world over together since 1968. he taught me how to sing and dance. He was a wonderful person.
— *Alex Spanos*

Epilogue
Friends of the Fox

The Friends of the Fox is a voluntary organization of individuals interested in preserving the memory and status of the Bob Hope/Fox California Theatre as a significant institution interwoven into the history and culture of Stockton. This organization began in December 1995, by people motivated to support the restoration and use of the theater which they believe is a key element in the revitalization of downtown Stockton. The board of directors actively assisted in the theater's conversion from a privately-owned building to one, first leased and then, owned by the City of Stockton. Its first President was local attorney Don Geiger (1995-1998) followed by Bonnie Mansfield (1998- 2001). The current President is Robert Hartzell.

When the city leased the Fox Theatre from owners Lawton and Merlo, it also entered into a management agreement with VenueTech, a company hired to manage the theater and bring in high-caliber entertainment. During this period the Friends of the Fox envisioned the theater as "The Crown Jewel," or centerpiece for the revitalizing process.

The Friends of the Fox, served as an advisory board when VenueTech presented various show options. This led to the creation of five or six shows grouped together and marketed as a "series". The packaged seasonal schedules were then used to entice the public to join the Friends of the Fox. There were several other member benefits, such as a discounted price for purchasing a majority of the shows in the series, seat selection and the option of retaining the same seat from season to season, and also an early bird discount package.

The organization grew to over 300 members when the board of directors created a "cultural growth fund" to underwrite performances by local entertainers. The fund has been successful in making contributions to the annual *Nutcracker Ballet* so that some less-privileged young people can attend this spectacular annual presentation.

One of the major obstacles was a perception that the downtown was unsafe. People were leery of venturing there in the evening. Also, many new to Stockton had never been to the heart of the city as there was no reason to go there. As a result, the Police Department increased their patrols of the downtown area, especially on show nights. Another major city effort was to keep the streets and sidewalks clean.

During the next five years, there were many outstanding performances. *Beach Blanket Babylon* was a huge success. This event included a sit-down dinner served in the front of the theater before the show. Other major successes were *Manhattan Transfer*, the *Moody Blues*, and the return of local entertainer Chris Issak.

In addition, there were a series of classic movies. However, the two 1950s vintage arc projectors required a complete overhaul and the sound system needed to be reinstalled before the movies could be shown. Volunteer Kenneth Walters repaired the projectors and three "Voice of the Theater" speakers were donated to the theater. The movies shown included *Psycho, Bride of Frankenstein, On Golden Pond, Ben Hur, It Happened One Night, Key Largo, How to Marry a Millionaire, Meet Me in St. Louis,* and *Laura.* As part of California's sesquicentennial celebration, The Friends of the Fox teamed up with the San Joaquin County Historical Society and presented *Sutter's Gold,* a movie about the 1845-1850 period in California's history.

In the summer of 2000, Bob Hartzell and Don Geiger discussed with the board of directors the idea of acquiring a theater pipe organ to replace the original one that had been removed in the 1950s. The theater needed a particularly powerful instrument for the size of the auditorium and because the size of the opening from the organ chambers were unusually small. They found the original Seattle Fox Theatre organ in storage in Southern California. The owners agreed to sell this Robert Morton pipe organ for $6,000 cash and a charitable in-kind donation of $20,000 to the Friends of the Fox. In addition, through another charitable contribution, the organization acquired components from the original Sacramento Senator Fox Theatre organ.

Under the direction of master organ technician David Moreno, twenty eight volunteers spent the next four and one half years restoring the organ. Geiger Manufacturing provided the working space, Union Planing Mill fabricated new wooden parts, and funding came through generous donations from foundations and individuals. By December of 2004, the organ restoration project was completed and it was installed in the theater. On April 10, 2005 the Friends of the Fox proudly presented an inaugural concert featuring noted organist Walter Strony. The plans are to use this massive organ for concerts, intermission entertainment as well as provide the background music for silent and classic movies. Fondly dubbed the

Courtesy of Dorothy Percival

Nutcracker Suite's Waltz of the Flowers stars Julia Armstrong Eck as the prima ballerina. This Christmas favorite has delighted Stocktonians for over twenty-five years. Below, the *Russian Trepak* dance featured (left to right) Nathan Woods, Curtis Greenwood, Jennifer Hastings and an unidentifiable dancer. Dance rehearsals begin in August and run until the three days of performances at Christmas time.

Courtesy of Dorothy Percival

Courtesy of Stephen Jester

The stage preparation for the
Moody Blues show.

Minnick Collection

The 1950s vintage projects were completely over-
hauled for the classic cinema films.

"Mighty Morton", this major contribution by the
Friends of the Fox will enhance the long term viability
of the theater.

In 2001, the theater got a new roof and an
upgraded air-condition system. Meanwhile, The
Friends of the Fox purchased a new popcorn machine,
brass stanchions and velvet ropes for the theater. In
addition, the organization concentrated on revamping

the upstairs lounge into a private reception room and
it became the setting for the *"Taste of Downtown" wine
reception.*

In January 2002, the theater was closed for
the major renovation. The 2,000-plus seats needed
repair and re-covering at a cost of $250 per seat.
The Friends of the Fox teamed with the Downtown
Stockton Alliance and the Greater Stockton Chamber

Minnick Collection

World-renowned organist, Walter Strony, performed an inaugural concert on the
Bob Hope Theatre's Robert Morton organ in April 2005. The event was sponsored by
the Friends of the Fox.

of Commerce for a major fund raising drive called "Save My Seat." For each $250 donation, a brass plaque bearing the name of the donor was affixed to the arm of the selected seat in perpetuity. The response from the community was gratifying in that, to date, almost 500 individuals and groups have "purchased" seats. This is a continuing Friends of the Fox project.

Minnick Collection

A September 2004 gala-re-opening of the Bob Hope/Fox California Theatre with performance by comedian Jerry Seinfeld drew a record crowd. Mrs. Bob Hope and Mr. and Mrs. Alex Spanos threw the switch to light up the marquee for the special dedication.

Minnick Collection

For the two years when the theater closed for the major renovation, the Friends of the Fox continued to meet monthly. City of Stockton officials reported on the theater's progress and periodically sought advice. On several occasions, The Friends of the Fox helped city officials resolve issues with the State Office of Historic Preservation and with the City of Stockton Cultural Heritage Board. There were also other meetings with city officials regarding the appropriate roles for the Friends of the Fox once the theater underwent a new management agreement with the private company, I.F.G. The Friends of the Fox agreed to:

- *Be recognized as the voluntary, public liaison body to the City of Stockton and theater management*

- *Create a docent program to train volunteers to give tours of the theater*
- *Present theater-oriented fund raising and community service events at the theater, such as classic and silent films, organ concerts, sale of CDs recorded on the "Mighty Morton", sale of a new Fox Theater history book, and other types of fund raising events or activities*
- *Continue to fund the existing "Cultural Growth Fund" and assist individuals and organizations who would otherwise not have access to the theater and its activities, and*
- *Publish a quarterly Friends of the Fox newsletter to promote membership and highlight coming attractions and activities at the theater*

The Friends of the Fox played a major role in t he September 18, 2004 reopening of the Bob Hope/ Fox California Theatre. A lavish dinner served in front of the theater on Main Street preceded the program headlining noted comedian Jerry Seinfeld. Friends of the Fox retained the services of Judith Buethe Public Relations to help plan the event and hired Cheri Ingram Enterprises to produce a video commemorating the many contributions of the theater's namesake, entertainer Bob Hope. It was a very successful event.

In 2005 The Friends of the Fox will help the Bob Hope/Fox California Theater celebrate its 75th birthday. Several plans are in the works for a commemorative event scheduled for October of 2005. There will also be a book on the history of the theater due out this Fall. The project is under the direction of historian/authoress Sylvia Sun Minnick with contributing chapters by Robert Shellenberger, Tom Bowe, D. Dennis Geiger, Marian Vieira Stevenson and many others.

To reiterate our mission and purpose, the Internal Revenue Service has designated Friends of the Fox as a 501(c)(3) (tax-exempt) organization. Members pay an annual dues. A sixteen-member board of directors conducts the business of the organization. It functions to establish programs and policies for the organization, maintains financial records and minutes of monthly meetings, and acts as a sounding board for theater management and City of Stockton officials. It sponsors and organizes various programs and activities to raise money to fund improvements at the theater.

We encourage those who are interested in the betterment of the theater and the revitalization of downtown Stockton to please join us.

Robert Hartzell

Epilogue
The Mighty Morton

The Golden Age of the movie palace was also the golden age of the mighty theatre organ. The moguls of the silent cinema built their palaces to enhance the experience of attending movies. From the beginning, the awful silence of their offerings almost immediately led to the use of music to add color and mood to enhance the performances. The use of pianos and small organs became common almost immediately. Improved and longer movies required more complex music. In the twenties, thirty piece symphony orchestras were often employed to match the quality of the screen offerings. Orchestra accompaniment was impossible for most small venues and expensive for all.

It was universally agreed a good organ and organist was preferable to a bad orchestra. A giant organ, capable of replacing the sound of a large orchestra answered the need. Basic large church organs quickly began to morph into a genre of their own. Talented musicians and tinkers steadily enhanced the great instruments so that they not only provided music with both power and grace, but also supplied the effects necessary to tell the story on the screen.

Roxie Theatre historian Ben M. Hall says it well:

The mighty Wurlitzer (and its counterparts) was as much a part of the movie palace as the electric lights that danced around the marquee, or the goldfish that swam in the lobby fountain. Inside the theatre the music seemed to bubble up and soar into the darkness of the balcony. Far below, bathed in a rose spotlight, was the organist perched in the maw of the great golden console. A flick of the finger, and chimes would call Ramona back beside the waterfall; a dramatic sweep of the hand and all would be silence save for the sobbing of the broken-hearted tibia languishing on the left loft as it was comforted by its mate, the crooning Vox Humana over on the right – to the tune of 'Prisoner of Love.' A quick kick at the crescendo pedal, and the mood would change to joy again – all glockenspiels, trumpets, tubas and snare drums – as an invisible McNamara's Band marched across the balcony.

The biggest organs were also a sound effects box, providing the performer with bells, whistles, sirens, tom-toms, rain on a tin roof, galloping horses, zithers and whatever else could be attached. (This trend, termed "glitzy," is demeaned by some theatre organ enthusiasts, and is evident today in pizza parlor instruments). Attending to all of these calls made the organist an acrobat as well as a musician. Organists were also performers in their own right, providing intermission and matinee concerts and leading community sings, all with style. And, very often, they were also the mechanics

Photos Courtesy of Stephen Jester

Photos courtesy of Stephen Jester

(Top and Right) A view of the various pipes and baffles in the organ chamber.

who spent their time between shows in the basement or in the lofts tuning, repairing and maintaining their instruments.

The traditional theater organ was an anachronism by the beginning of World War II. They no longer served the purpose of establishing mood and carrying the story line as they had in the days of the silents.

COMPONENTS OF THE "MIGHTY MORTON"

RANKS (sets of pipes)	PERCUSSIONS	EFFECTS
1 – English Horn	1 – Piano (midi)	1 – Police Siren
2 – Trumpet	2 – Vibraphone (midi)	2 – Police Whistle
3 – Tuba	3 – Marimba/Harp	3 – Ships Bell
4 – Diapason	4 – Chrysoglott	4 – Door Bell
5 – Tibia Clausa	5 – Orchestra Bells	5 – Surf
6 – Tibia Minor	6 – Xylophone	6 – Train Whistle
7 – Kinura	7 – Cathedral Chimes	7 – Wolf Whistle
8 – Orchestral Oboe	**TRAPS**	8 – Boat Whistle
9 – Krumet	Bass Drum	9 – Bird Call I
10 – Clarinet	Kettle Drum	10 – Bird Call II
11 – Oboe Horn	Snare Drum	11 – Horse Hooves
12 – Gamba	Tom Tom	12 – Auto Horn
13 – Violin	Chinese Wood Drum	13 – Fire Gong
14 – Violin Celeste I	Crash Cymbal	14 – Thunder
15 – Violin Celeste II	Tap Cymbal	
16 – Viola	Jazz Cymbal	
17 – Harmonic Flute	Cymbal Roll	
18 – Concert Flute	Tambourine	
19 – Flute Celeste	Castanets	
20 – Solo Vox Humana	Triangle	
21 – Vox Humana	Sleigh Bells	

They sat idle or were dismantled and stored away. According to organ authority Robert Hartzell, the theater organ was saved from oblivion by the invention of high fidelity recording techniques and stereophonic sound, and by the records of George Wright. The new technology made it possible to, at last, record the full sound and color and excitement of the true theater organ, and Wright provided the artistry. His recordings and concerts provided a new audience and led to the rebirth of the mighty theatre organ.

Stockton's first noted theater organ was a Wurlitzer Automatic Organ installed at the Idle Hour in 1910. When the T&D was opened in 1917 it featured a fine 9 rank Wurlitzer which was later removed and installed in the new Fox California in 1930. It was expanded by addition of Morton pipes from the Tivoli Theatre in San Francisco. It was sold in the 1950s and has disappeared. As a replacement, Friends of the Fox found and purchased, a Robert Morton organ originally installed in the Seattle Fox in 1928. Devoted volunteers spent thousands of man-hours restoring the Morton, and with the addition of five additional ranks, it is a superb instrument, worthy of its new home.

It is fitting that the resurrected Fox, now the Bob Hope, should have an organ of its own, worthy of its new setting. And it does.

Robert Shellenberger

Minnick Collection

Four annual consoles are installed in the orchestra pit and mounted on a hydraulic organ lift.
Wind Supply created by 15-horsepower turbine blower, located in the theater basement.
The entire organ is controlled by computer designed by Rickman Uniflex Systems of Reno, Nevada.

Epilogue
Ghost Light:
A Returning Tradition

During the compilation for this book, there were tidbits of information that piqued my interest particularly when mentioned by a variety of sources and when these people's experiences at the Fox California spanned several decades. This curious topic involves the sensing of some spiritual presence or presences, aberrations, in other word, ghosts. These are the courses of conversation, which you, the reader, might decipher for yourself:

Brian Farnsworth (Edward Merlo's handyman at the Fox from 1978 to 1998):

…More than once I felt some type of presence and in more than one place. There was something in the basement where the main exhaust/blower funneled into the tunnels in front of the building. I sensed some type of pressure there in what we called the "tombs." Going up stairs to the mezzanine and where the walls begin to curve near the drinking fountain, I felt I was often followed. There was a cold feeling near me. I learned to start a conversation, even though I was talking to myself. I would say aloud where I was going and what I was going to do. If I was in a hurry and don't say anything I guess I was acting disrespectful. During those times there was a tap on my shoulder, and, even once, a slap on my forehead. Other fellows working at the Fox also had similar experiences and I've suggested to them that they, too, need to keep the spirit informed about their doings.

Guillermo Rodriquez (Jessie Marquez's projectionist 1975-78):

Some nights I worked all alone in the projection booth. At closing I turned off all the power and walked all the way down to the lobby, sometimes with and sometimes without a flashlight. I could feel someone walking behind me, especially when going down from the projectionist booth stairs and then again in the middle section of the lobby near the office on the right side. I especially heard some type of noise on the mezzanine level next to the office on the right side.

David Marquez

My mother also remembered my father coming out rather quickly from the stage area when he turned the lights off in that area because he felt a strong presence. There were two areas that we know of – the stage and the balcony – when there was a presence.

Ric Gauuan (a director for Hunter Square Acting Company):

We rehearsed upstairs in the mezzanine area and after rehearsal we cleared the area very quickly. We felt spooked out, it was weird.

Kelly White Keagy (volunteer usher 2005):

Just to let you know, the upstairs balcony area is haunted. I don't know about downstairs. The people who work down there haven't seen or felt anything. But all of us upstairs have experienced something.

My "Phantom" likes to hang around at the top of the stairs in the upper balcony. A couple of times he/she pats my back or my shoulder as if to tell me to move, or to say, "Isn't that great?" When this happens, it gets really cold around me. Others have seen a gentleman sitting in the back row on the "even" side. One minute he's there, the next he's gone. Down in the lower balcony in the area where the railing is to the far right "someone" is there.

Stephen Jester (technical director 2005)

It seems before every show something goes wrong with the electrical or some other system. It has never failed, even to this day. The glitch is often only momentarily.

Admittedly, not everyone who has worked there have felt or sensed any type of presence. However, when asked, other individuals are not surprised. Is there a ghostly presence at the Fox? Given the age of the Bob Hope/Fox California Theatre, I would be disappointed if our theater did not have its full complement of theater traditions and folklore.

One such performing theater tradition is to have a "ghostlight" on stage. It should not be anything fancy, no lamp shade, nothing high tech or state-of-the-art, and nothing high powered. Superstition has it that if a theater "goes dark" it would mean bad luck. A reasonable explanation for the small light is to allow actors and employees to leave without falling into the orchestra pit. However, there are other tales such as the light will draw all the ghosts toward the stage instead of having them wandering around the theater. Another myth is that the light will signal the ghosts that it was their turn on the stage.

The Marquez family had never heard of this theater tradition. Did the Bob Hope/Fox California ever have a ghostlight? Yes, accordingly, it was an ugly, gooseneck lamp but has since disappeared. With the renovation and under the management of I.F.G., a new ghostlight has again become part of the theater tradition. It is a 1930s-vintage floor lamp on casters, without a lamp shade. It is parked to the side during performances and takes center stage on cue.

Tradition is alive and well.

Sylvia Sun Minnick

The Bob Hope/Fox California Ghostlight.

Acknowledgements

EDWARD J. CHAVEZ
Mayor

GARY S. GIOVANETTI
Vice Mayor
District 5

Stockton
All-America City
2004
1999

CITY OF STOCKTON

OFFICE OF THE CITY COUNCIL

CITY HALL • 425 N. El Dorado Street • Stockton, CA 95202-1997
209/937-8244 • Fax 209/937-8568

STEVE J. BESTOLARIDES
District 1

DAN J. CHAPMAN
District 2

LESLIE BARANCO MARTIN
District 3

CLEM LEE
District 4

REBECCA G. NABORS
District 6

June 3, 2005

We and the rest of Stockton's citizens are pleased to be sharing in this Seventy-Fifth Anniversary celebration of the Bob Hope/Fox California Theatre. This commemorative book STOCKTON'S CROWN JEWEL: The Bob Hope/Fox California is a true testimony to the spirit of Stockton's people and the legacy of downtown.

As natives in this wonderful city, the theatre has been very much a vital part of our boyhood years. Our own personal memories of Saturday matinees, evening dates and camaraderie that we shared with our friends at the Fox will be forever cherished.

Although our theatre fell into disrepair through years and wear-and-tear, saving this theatre and restoring it to its original elegance have lend to our commitment to revitalize the downtown. Congratulate yourself STOCKTONIANS!

EDWARD J. CHAVEZ
MAYOR

GARY PODESTO
FORMER MAYOR

www.stocktongov.com
Population: 263,000 +

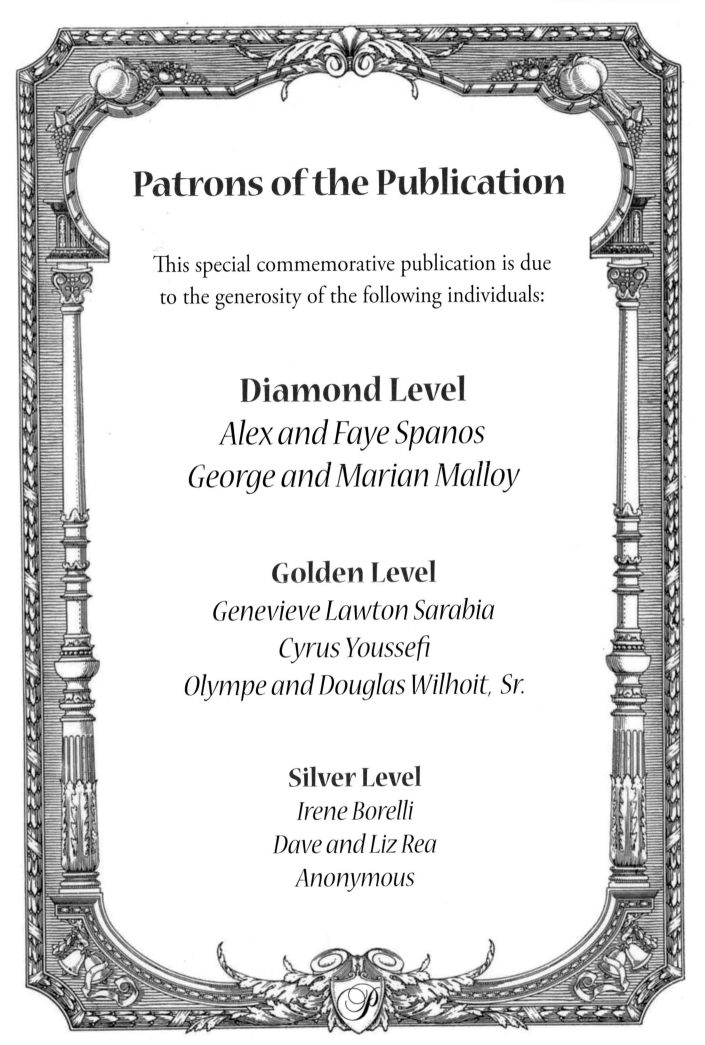

Patrons of the Publication

This special commemorative publication is due
to the generosity of the following individuals:

Diamond Level

Alex and Faye Spanos

George and Marian Malloy

Golden Level

Genevieve Lawton Sarabia

Cyrus Youssefi

Olympe and Douglas Wilhoit, Sr.

Silver Level

Irene Borelli

Dave and Liz Rea

Anonymous

Community Resources, Oral Tradition and Archival Repository

This has been an effort of not one but many. We, authors, are grateful to the Friends of the Fox for their vision in choosing this book as a way to celebrate the 75th anniversary of the Bob Hope/Fox California Theatre. We are indebted to the following people who shared their memories, photos and memorabilia. Others spent time researching, typing, editing, proofreading and cheering us on. Our thanks to:

Florence Strecher Allen, Don Babcock, Margie Baldwin, Dolores Rimassa Belew, Carol Bell, Marilyn "Dodie" Bettencourt, Irene Borelli, Carol Burns, Lily Wong Chin, Evelyn Cintola, Lex Corrales, Dan De Angelis, Dean and Erma DeCarli, Mike DeLorenzo, Gladys Adams DePauli, Ann and Frank Esau, Kevin Falls, Brian Farnsworth, Margaret Van Vranken Ficovich, Mike Fitzgerald, June Frey, Greg Folsom, Ric Gauuan, LaVerne Ghiorzo, Ward Grant, Stuart Greenbaum, Dennis Halm, Jill Bennett Heard, Dorothy Trachiotis Henning, Barbara Herenden, Yvonne DuBois Hill, John Hinson, Joe Holt, Gladys Ikeda, Marian Jacobs, Stephen Jester, Kathleen Bennett Johnson, Sharon and Tom Kellogg, Frank Kim, Lydia Kim, John Klose, Lyn Krieger, Ann Gallo Lina, Clarence Louie, Eva Low, Roveta June Bertram Madding, Betty and Del McComb, David Marquez, Greg Massei, Bill Maxwell, Greg Meadows, Kathy Meissner, Thor Minnick, Steve Morales, Carolyn Eproson Mortenson, Dorothy Mulvihill, Natalia Orfanos, Dorothy Percival, Gary Podesto, Becky Lina Potten, Sally Praegitzer, Bob Price, Ben Reddish, Dorothy Curtis Rollins, Lori Rosales, Tod Ruhstaller, Dan Sanchez, Genevieve Lawton Sarabia, Debbie Scott, Alvin Sibell, Jerry Sola, Bob Snyder, Tom Shephard, Elizabeth Steele, Gail Weldy Traverso, Ed Van Vranken, Jim Watson, Douglas and Olympe Wilhoit, Sr., Doug Wilhoit, Jr., Gayla Wilson and Jim Yost

We appreciate the courtesy, helpfulness and generosity of the following institutions and their staff: Bank of Stockton, Caesar Chavez Library, Haggin Museum, San Joaquin County Historical Museum, Stockton Chamber of Commerce, City of Stockton City Clerk's Office, City of Stockton City Manager's Office and the staff at the Bob Hope Theatre.

The Mighty Morton Donors and Volunteers

There are two "Ms" to any project – money and muscles. Both are equally important and have the same timing priority. The Bob Hope/Fox California Theater is extremely fortunate that those involved with the Robert Morton organ or rather the "Mighty Morton" project were endowed also with vision and avocation. Tenacity was also thrown into the mix.

Monetary and in-kind contributions came from the following foundations, companies and individuals. The funds were funneled through the Friends of the Fox as well as to the City of Stockton and assigned to the Friends of the Fox specifically for the organ project. We are grateful to:

The American Theatre Organ Society, The Capecchio Foundation, The Ross and Marilyn Bewley Charitable Foundation, Inc., Wendell Jacob, Leroy Buller, DDS., Builders Exchange of Stockton Foundation, Bloom Construction, F & H Construction, Roek Construction, F & M Bank, Bank of Agriculture and Commerce, Bert Atwood, Union Planing Mill, Bonnie and Tuilio Ciauri, Nor-Cal Theatre Organ Society, Neumiller & Beardslee, Madrina Smith, Robert and Eleanor Lawrence, Lockeford True Value Hardware, Delta Plating, Dennis Donald Geiger, Kenneth Walters, Jack Klein Trust Partnership, Thompson Bros., A.F. Toccoli and Sons and The Grupe Company.

Thirty-four individuals, men and women, from cities as far away as San Jose, Rio Vista, Colfax, Glencoe, Antelope Citrus Heights, Carmichael, Orange, Fair Oaks, Sacramento, Lodi, Stockton, Morada and Ripon, faithfully showed up on Mondays, week after week, at the Geiger Manufacturing Plant. They put in thousands of man hours calculating, separating, building, piecing and tying together and polishing the Mighty Morton. Each lent his own expertise. Thank you to:

Mike DeLorenzo, Verna Blain, Don Hawkinson, Gerge Byrd, Maxine Padilla, Jim and Emilia Seiferling, Bob Lemon, Bob Hartzell, Don Siefert, Leroy Buller, Don Burford, John Carelton, Barbara and Beverley Harris, Bert Kuntz, Warren Lubich, Dave Moreno, Tom Norvell, Craig Peterson, Mac Wurtzbaugh, Tom Thompson, Jeff Thompson, John Thompson, Don Croom, Michael Lapalusa, Matias Bombal, Ron Teunissen, Ward Johnson, Matthew Haack, Roger Haack, Art Nisson, Don Near, and Reed and Renee Robbins.

Courtesy of Jodee Samuelsen

Donors and volunteers gathered to celebrate the inauguration of the Mighty Morton on April 23, 2005.

The Renovation Efforts

Kudos to everyone involved in the renovation efforts: those who made major financial contributions, others who lent their artistic and architectural talent, and still others in the private sector and city staff who add their own touches and expertise to restore Stockton's CROWN JEWEL. To them, our community is extremely grateful.

DONORS:

A.G. Spanos

Bank of Stockton

Carl Thompson

The Grupe Company

Toccoli Limited Partnership

The Record

ARCHITECT:

Wenell Mattheis Bowe Architects

CONTRACTOR:

McFadden Construction

OTHER CONTRACTORS AND MAJOR SUBCONTRACTORS:

EverGreene Painting Studios, Inc.

Myklebust Sears

Applegate-Johnson, Inc.

Fernando Duarte Design/Alpha Signs
   of Sacramento

American Seating Company

Pinasco Plumbing and Heating.

Auerbach and Associates

HCS Engineering, Inc.

Deek Productions LLC

CLT

Architectural Resources Group

Roof Systems Engineering

CAL, Inc.

Hazard Management Service

JJ Floor Covering, Inc.

B & R Roofing

Safway Steel Products, Inc.

Cole Yee Schubert

Stagecraft Industries, Inc.

Rogers & Associates, Inc.

BBI Engineering, Inc.

CITY STAFF: From the very beginning to the last finite touches, city employees stayed the course and to them go the greatest recognition:

John Austin, Patrick Bickham, George Cabrera, Jay Coffey, John Connally, Alice Duer, Harold Duncan, Jason Ender, Greg Folsom, Bob Fuson, Jim Glaser, Terrie Henderson, John Hinson, Lyn Krieger, Lorre Islas, Anthony Keith, Gordon MacKay, Laurie Montes, Dwane Milnes, Tom Meath, Ben Nozuka, Gene Painchaud, Tom Polina, Deserie Schaffer, Roy Severson, Tam Serverson, Bob Sivell, Roger Storey, Ed Tofanelli, Kathy Tomura and Bill Watson.

Bibliography

Bancroft, Hubert Howe. *History of California*. Vols. I to VII. San Francisco: 1886-1890.

Bennett, Mel. *Stockton's Theatre of Yesterday*. Aptos, CA: Willow House, 1979.

Benton, Vicki Lee. *A History of the Fox California Theater* (Paper for History 10, San Joaquin Delta College). 1974.

Hall, Ben M., and Bosley Crowther. *The Remaining Best Seats*. New York: Bramwell House, 1959.

Kennedy, Glenn. *It Happened In Stockton*. Private printing (typescript).

Martin, V. Covert. *Stockton Album*. Stockton: 1959.

Noid, Benjamin Maynord. *History of Theatre in Stockton, California 1850-1892*. University of Utah, Ph.D. dissertation 1968.

Stockton Daily Independent

The Stockton Record

Tinkham, George H. *History of San Joaquin County, California*. San Francisco: Historic Record Co., 1923.

Tinkham, George H. *History of Stockton*. W.M. Hinton & Co., 1980.

STAGE HOUSE

STAGE DIMENSIONS

Stage Width:	78' clear from fly rail stage right to stage left wall
Stage Depth:	28' 4" clear from smoke pocket to face of rear wall pilasters.
Fixed Stage Apron:	5' 0" depth from face of main drapery to edge of orchestra pit.
Pit Filler Platform System:	8' 11" (at apex) upstage to downstage distance.
Orchestra Pit:	5' 3" depth from stage floor (3' apron overhang). Organ lift allows deployment of organ from storage location to "play position"

FLY SYSTEM

Single purchase counterweight:	30 total lines, primarily 8" on centers
Dedicated electric truss battens:	5
General purpose battens:	56' long, 1.5" schedule 40 black pipe
Loading capacity:	(live load/arbor space) per batten approximately 25LBS/linear ft.

STAGE FLOOR

Existing wood floor:	Set on sleepers not resiliently mounted or sprung, 100 PSF

BACKSTAGE

LOADING DOCK

Loading door:	At stage level (stage left), incline to street level (Market) and corner to negotiate.
	Approximately 30' from street downhill to stage loading doors.
Loading Door Dimensions:	7' 8.5" wide, 11' tall.
Access to House Level:	From street (Market) to house level (house left) approximately 69' 9" with minimum door dimensions 3' 6" wide and 6' 6" tall.
Access to House Level:	San Joaquin street entrance with minimum door dimensions 5' wide and 6' 7.5" tall.

TRUCK/PARKING

Street only:	No direct loading to stage.

WARDROBE

No washer/dryer facilities.	No direct loading to dressing rooms (stairs).

DRESSING ROOMS

3 dressing rooms each have 10 mirrors w/ lights and counters.

Dressing room 1:	26' x 12' with access to bathroom and shared shower
Dressing room 2:	31' x 8' only accessible from dressing room 1
Dressing room 3:	30' x 10' with access to bathroom and shared shower

ELECTRICS

PERMANENT DIMMING SYSTEM

130-2.4 kw ETC dimmers, Express48/96 console

All circuits "stagepin" 3-pin (2P&G type), 20 amps

Distributed DMX lines w/patch bay & splitter

Control Locations at Projection Booth, mid house rehearsal position, back of house mix (under balcony)

ONSTAGE LIGHTING POSITIONS

Electrics (5 total)

Electrics #1:	12 circuits
Electrics #2:	12 circuits
Electrics #3:	12 circuits
Electrics #4:	12 circuits
Electrics #5:	18 circuits

FLOOR POCKETS

3 boxes each with 3 Circuit Stage Left

3 boxes each with 3 Circuit Stage Right

FRONT OF HOUSE LIGHTING POSITIONS/CIRCUITS

Catwalk 27 Circuits

Balcony Front 3 Circuits

House Left Box 8 Circuits

House Right Box 8 Circuits

Projection Booth 2 Strong Xenon Super Trooper 2K spot lights

TOURING POWER ONSTAGE

2 400amp per leg service, both stage right

1 300amp per leg service stage right

1 100amp per leg service stage left

SOUND

FOH REINFORCEMENT AND MONITOR SYSTEM

Mix position at back of house under balcony 9' x 24' level surface

Sound Boards: 40 channel Yamaha PM3000 FOH sound console

1 PM3000 PSU

40 channel Ramsa 840 MON sound console

1 840 PSU

SNAKES

1 230' 40 channel audio snake w/splitter

4 9 channel sub snakes

SPEAKERS & MONITORS

Meyers Speaker Arrays: 1 house left, 1 house right

Top: 2 Meyers MSL-3 and 1 DS-2

Bottoms: 2 Meyers MSL-3 and 1 DS-2

8 Meyers UM1B stage wedges

3 Meyers UPA1C fill speakers

4 Meyers 650-R2 sub speakers

DELAY SPEAKERS SYSTEM

6 EAW JF-80 under balcony

3 EAW JF-80 over balcony

4 EAW JF-80 at stage lip

MICROPHONES

4 SM81 condenser	4 SM58
4 MD-421 Senn.	1 D112
4 SM57	7 D.I.'s

COMMUNICATIONS

INTERCOM

2 channel Clear-Com

PROGRAM/PAGE

Program monitors in dressing rooms with page capability.

ASSISTIVE LISTENING

FM, fed from independent microphone

VIDEO

VIDEO SYSTEM

1 Video screen 39' 3" Wide and 17' tall. (on batten)

Dry video lines and patch bays only.

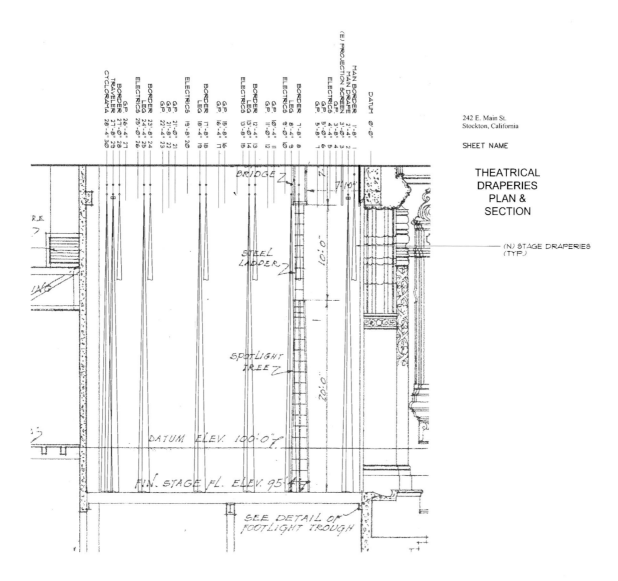

242 E. Main St.
Stockton, California

SHEET NAME

**THEATRICAL
DRAPERIES
PLAN &
SECTION**

———— (N) STAGE DRAPERIES
(TYP.)

(2) SECTION AT BATTENS
¼" = 1'-0"

GENERAL NOTES

1. ALL FASTENERS TO HAVE LOCKWASHERS OR OTHER APPROVED
   SELF-LOCKING HARDWARE.

2. ALL EXPOSED ELEMENTS TO BE FINISHED FLAT BLACK UNLESS
   NOTED OTHERWISE.

3. RIGGING CONTRACTOR TO VERIFY ALL DIMENSIONS AND
   CONDITIONS IN FIELD.

4. ALL EQUIPMENT BY RIGGING CONTRACTOR UNLESS
   NOTED OTHERWISE.

5. RIGGING CONTRACTOR TO VERIFY ALL MOTOR SIZES,
   LOADS, POWER REQUIREMENTS, AND CONTROL WIRE SIZES AND COUNTS.

6. ALL CONDUIT, WIRE, POWER FEEDS, JUNCTION/PULL BOXES AND FINAL
   TERMINATIONS (UNDER ELECTRICAL)

7. NO CONDUIT OR CONDUIT SUPPORTS PERMITTED ON HORIZONTAL PIPES
   OR CATWALK RAILINGS. ALL CATWALK RAILINGS TO BE COMPLETELY
   CLEAR OF ALL OBSTRUCTIONS FROM TOP OF KICK PLATE TO TOP OF
   UPPER HORIZONTAL RAILING.

8. THIS DRAWING IS INTENDED TO PROVIDE INFORMATION REGARDING
   THEATRICAL EQUIPMENT ONLY. REFER TO APPLICABLE ARCHITECTURAL
   OR ENGINEERING DRAWINGS FOR ARCHITECTURAL AND ENGINEERING
   INFORMATION RELATING TO THE BUILDING.

Index

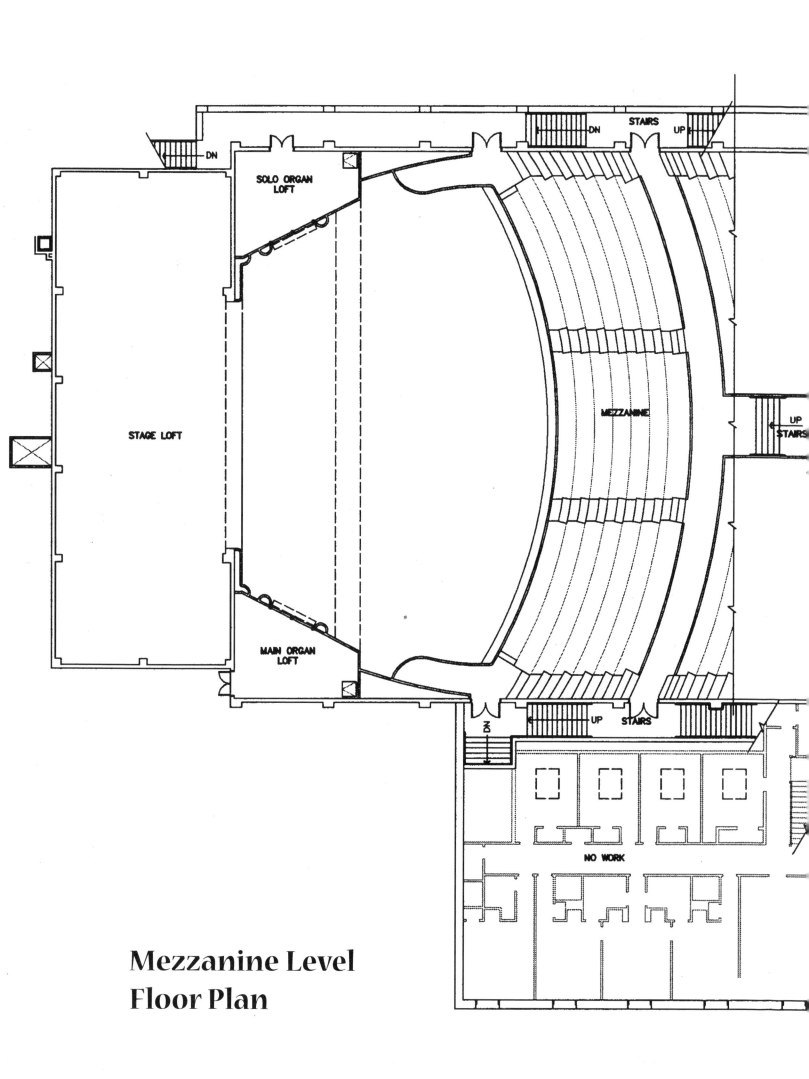

DN

SOLO ORGAN
LOFT

STAGE LOFT

MAIN ORGAN
LOFT

DN

DN STAIRS UP

MEZZANINE

UP
STAIRS

UP STAIRS

NO WORK

**Mezzanine Level
Floor Plan**